T0339559

Cambridge Elements ≡

Elements in Corpus Linguistics
edited by
Susan Hunston
University of Birmingham

COLLOCATIONS, CORPORA AND LANGUAGE LEARNING

Paweł Szudarski
University of Nottingham

Shaftesbury Road, Cambridge CB2 8EA, United Kingdom

One Liberty Plaza, 20th Floor, New York, NY 10006, USA

477 Williamstown Road, Port Melbourne, VIC 3207, Australia

314–321, 3rd Floor, Plot 3, Splendor Forum, Jasola District Centre,
New Delhi – 110025, India

103 Penang Road, #05–06/07, Visioncrest Commercial, Singapore 238467

Cambridge University Press is part of Cambridge University Press & Assessment,
a department of the University of Cambridge.

We share the University's mission to contribute to society through the pursuit of
education, learning and research at the highest international levels of excellence.

www.cambridge.org
Information on this title: www.cambridge.org/9781108994798

DOI: 10.1017/9781108992602

First published 2023

A catalogue record for this publication is available from the British Library.

ISBN 978-1-108-99479-8 Paperback
ISSN 2632-8097 (online)
ISSN 2632-8089 (print)

Collocations, Corpora and Language Learning

Elements in Corpus Linguistics

DOI: 10.1017/9781108992602
First published online: June 2023

Paweł Szudarski
University of Nottingham

Author for correspondence: Paweł Szudarski, pawel.szudarski@
nottingham.ac.uk

Abstract: This Element provides a systematic overview and synthesis of corpus-based research into collocations focusing on the learning and use of collocations by second language (L2) users. Underlining the importance of collocation as a key notion within the field of corpus linguistics, the text offers a state-of-the-art account of the main findings related to the applications of corpora and corpus-based measures for defining, identifying and analysing collocations as related to second language acquisition. Emphasising the quality of L2 collocation research, the Element illustrates key methodological issues to be considered when conducting this type of corpus analysis. It also discusses examples of pertinent research questions and points to representative studies treated as models of good practice. Aiming at researchers both new and experienced, the Element also points to avenues for future work and shows the relevance of corpus-based analysis for improving the process of learning and teaching of L2 collocations.

Keywords: collocation, corpus analysis of collocations, learning collocations in a second language, corpora and phraseology, formulaic language

ISBNs: 9781108994798 (PB), 9781108992602 (OC)
ISSNs: 2632-8097 (online), 2632-8089 (print)

Contents

1 Introduction

The last few decades have seen an impressive growth of interest in corpus-based analysis of language. Corpora, large computerised collections of language data, have been instrumental in the expansion of many subdisciplines within linguistics, and it is fair to say that corpus methods have become an indispensable tool for much of contemporary linguistic research. In fact, in appraising the impact of corpora on the way linguistic analysis is currently carried out, some authors (e,, Hanks, 2012; Chambers, 2019) have gone as far as stating that corpora have revolutionised language studies by providing a whole new range of methods and tools to study language, its learning and use across varied settings and contexts (see also O'Keeffe & McCarthy, 2022, for a summary of the evolution of corpus linguistics in the last ten years).

Examples of areas where corpora have proved highly useful are plentiful and include, among others, corpus-assisted discourse analysis, register and genre variation studies, second language acquisition (SLA) and applied corpus-based research. This Element focuses on the last two, underlining the importance of corpora for exploring collocations as a type or category of the broader phenomenon of formulaic language (see Section 2.1 for an overview). Specifically, the discussion centres on corpus-based and corpus-informed analyses of collocations treated as frequently recurring two-to-three-word lexical units characterised by relative transparency of meaning and restricted connectedness of the constituent words (e.g., 'make an error' as opposed to 'do an error'). In particular, the Element demonstrates the pivotal role of corpora in analysing collocations as related to second language (L2) research, offering a critical synthesis of the current findings and pointing to key methodological considerations that affect the quality and validity of collocation studies.

My intention as the author of this text has been to provide a useful account of the main concepts and debates in the field, not only by presenting the most pertinent research questions and examples of studies in this line of inquiry but also by discussing the key methodological decisions that need to be made in carrying out this type of corpus-based work. By overviewing the main traditions and approaches followed in collocation studies, the Element seeks to present specific methods and types of analysis, explaining how corpus data, methods and tools are particularly effective at delving into the varied ways in which words co-occur and collocate as phraseological partnerships. In this sense then, *Corpora, Collocation and Language Learning* has been conceptualised as a specialised but accessible introduction to corpus-based collocation research, aimed at both fellow linguists interested in studying the phenomenon of collocations but also language practitioners who may want to turn to corpora as a way of addressing practical challenges linked to selecting and teaching examples of specific word pairs deemed important for L2 pedagogy.

In practical terms, this means that by the end of the Element, the reader should have a thorough theoretical understanding of collocations as a key concept in corpus linguistics. They should also be well versed in the mechanics and methodologies associated with corpus-based analyses of collocations, enabling the pursuit of questions like the following:

- How do we define and identify different types of collocations?
- Which collocations are used more often in learner language or academic language?
- What is the relationship between the frequency of occurrence and the learning of collocations? What other factors affect this process?
- How is the learning and use of collocations by advanced L2 learners different from that by intermediate-level learners?
- What is the relationship between the use of collocations and the assessment of L2 learners' proficiency?
- How can corpus research inform the process of L2 teaching and materials development so that learners are provided with the optimal conditions for learning collocations?
- What aspects of L2 learning and teaching can benefit from the affordances of corpus analysis?

With these questions serving as the starting point, the Element is divided into five sections. Following this Introduction, Section 2 focuses on defining the term 'collocation', situating it in the literature on the broader phenomenon of formulaic language and explaining how corpora have been pivotal in advancing the understanding of this topic. Section 3 is an overview of the main corpus methods and tools that can be applied to the study of collocations. By discussing aspects of corpus analysis and presenting representative corpus-based studies, the aim of this section is to show how to search for examples of collocations in corpora, apply different corpus-based measures and statistical tests of word partnerships and analyse the use of collocations by taking multiple research perspectives. Building on this, Section 4 lies at the heart of this Element and provides a selection of corpus-based studies into L2 collocational learning and teaching, focusing specifically on learner corpora and a variety of factors that affect the acquisition and use of collocations by first and second language (L1 and L2, respectively) speakers. Linking corpus insights with findings from SLA, psycholinguistics and language pedagogy, this section showcases key findings in L2 collocation research, presents exemplary studies which model how to draw on corpora and discusses the practical implications of this work for language education. Finally, Section 5 offers a summary of the Element and recognises contributions and recent developments within corpus-based analysis in terms of advancing collocation studies and applied linguistics research more broadly. Using the reviewed findings, the discussion concludes with reflections on the evolution of the field, emphasises the instrumental role of corpora in studying collocations as a crucial aspect of language and describes possible avenues for future empirical work.

To aid the reading process, the Element includes a number of features whose aim is to not only enhance the reader's understanding of the main issues but also to invite them to critically engage with the existing collocation studies and consider the numerous methodological choices that need to be made as corpus analysis is undertaken. One such feature is quotations presented throughout the text, which illustrate the main points being discussed; another is study boxes which report relevant findings from corpus-based studies and model best practice in carrying out collocation analysis. Further, considering the current popularity of corpus-based work into the collocability of words and L2 phraseology, the Element also references many examples of studies which can be consulted for further information, with a view to encouraging readers to engage with the wider literature, immerse in the richness of corpus-based inquiry and embark on their own journey in this fast-growing area of linguistic analysis.

Finally, it is also worth adding that while the Element centres on collocations (e.g., 'make a mistake', 'strong coffee', 'extenuating circumstances'), where relevant, the discussion also draws on the wider spectrum of corpus-based work into formulaic sequences broadly defined as 'multiword phenomena which holistically represent a single meaning or function' (Wood, 2020, p. 30). In such cases, it is clearly indicated which types of phrases or formulaic units are being referred to, with explanations provided on how specific types of corpus-based analyses contribute to broadening our understanding of word co-occurrence, formulaicity and phraseological patterning.

2 How Are Collocations Defined?

2.1 Collocations and Formulaic Language

In the last thirty years or so, there has been a great deal of attention paid to collocations as a key element of language, with important developments in corpus analysis resulting in a multitude of new research focused on vocabulary studies (Szudarski, 2018; Granger, 2021; Durrant et al., 2022; Szudarski & Barclay, 2022). Thanks to the advent of corpora, it has become clear that language is highly patterned and to a large extent consists of fixed vocabulary and phraseological units, including not only collocations but also idioms ('red herring'), binomials ('ladies and gentlemen'), lexical bundles as contiguous sequences of words that recur in speech and writing ('it is important that') and other types of phrases (for a useful discussion of research into such multi-word units, see Siyanova-Chanturia & Omidian, 2020). In fact, the discovery that multi-word units are ubiquitous in natural language has been one of the major contributions of corpora to the field (Forsberg Lundell, 2021), bringing a new vitality to lexical studies and resulting in 'a complete overhaul of the theory and practice of phraseology' (Granger, 2021, p. 5).

With this in mind, this section focuses on questions related to defining collocations, recognising the importance of corpora in identifying relations between collocating words and explaining also how collocation studies need to be considered within the broader context of corpus-based research. That said, while this Element is very much grounded in the wider discussion devoted to the formulaicity of language, it is important to note that its goal is not to provide a detailed review of the vast literature devoted to this topic (for a comprehensive account, see Siyanova-Chanturia & Pellicer-Sanchez, 2019; see also Schmitt, 2022 for a useful summary). Rather, after this introductory section, the remainder of the text is concerned predominantly with collocations treated as a type of formulaic language, with examples of specific pairs of words identified according to both phraseology- and corpus-based criteria (for details, see Section 2.4).

In terms of the structure of this section, the paragraphs that follow first present collocation as a central concept in corpus linguistics, with Section 2.2 relating collocation research to Sinclair's idiom principle and the terminological challenges besetting this area of work. Next, the importance of corpora is underscored, highlighting their role in studying the graded and probabilistic nature of collocations as observed in the lexical and lexico-grammatical partnerships they form (Section 2.3). Crucially, whilst individual language users can identify such partnerships in informal and intuitive ways, it is also true that their subjective intuitions and predictions might turn out to be inaccurate or inconsistent. For instance, when it comes to rating lower-frequency words and phrases, research points to variation in the consistency and accuracy of responses amongst both L1 and L2 speakers (Schmitt & Dunham, 1999; Alderson, 2007; Siyanova-Chanturia & Spina, 2015). This is where the power of corpora comes to the fore, with Section 2.4 describing the main traditions followed in collocation research and introducing a range of measures used in corpus-based studies. Not only do they allow us to measure collocations in a reliable and automatic way but they also help to tap into different dimensions of word co-occurrence, throwing light on the intricate ways and relations between collocating words. Yet another dimension of collocation studies is tackled in Section 2.5, which makes a distinction between the textual and the psycholinguistic reality of collocations.

2.2 Collocations as a Central Concept, Idiom Principle and Terminological Challenges

A great deal of corpus-based research into collocations has been inspired by the pioneering work of John Sinclair, one of the key figures in establishing corpus linguistics as a new research paradigm and method of analysis. Based on the 1980s work on the COBUILD Corpus, Sinclair (1991) proposed that language and its use are governed by two main principles: the open-choice principle, in which speakers are unrestricted in their linguistic choices and construct sentences by selecting words item by item; and the idiom principle, according to which speakers and writers construct sentences and utterances by means of 'ready-made' phrases, collocations and phraseological chunks. This Element focuses on the latter, putting collocations at the centre of language analysis and highlighting their role in L2 learning and use.

Quote 1
Firth (1957, p. 179) 'You shall know a word by the company it keeps.'

When it comes to research, Sinclair and his followers have been less preoccupied with setting clear boundaries and determining whether phraseology is concerned more with lexis or grammar. Rather, they have emphasised the pervasiveness of collocations and other types of word combinations, stressing the part such phraseological units play in conveying specific meanings and fulfilling important pragmatic functions. This, for instance, includes phrases that express speakers' stance or attitudinal meanings (for details on discourse functions performed by collocations and phraseological units, see Schmitt & Carter, 2004; O'Keeffe et al., 2007; Carter, 2012; see also Durrant & Mathews-Aydinli, 2011 for details on a function-first approach to the identification of important phrases). Put differently, corpus-based accounts of phraseology have emphasised the idiom principle and the concept of lexico-grammar (O'Keeffe et al., 2007; Römer, 2009; Szudarski, 2018). In this approach, rather than seen as two separate levels of language, grammar and lexis are intrinsically intertwined (Granger, 2021), with recurrent collocations and lexico-grammatical patterns occupying a central position and reflecting a distinct psycholinguistic reality of phrases in speakers' mental lexicons (see Section 2.5 for details on Hoey's (2005) notion of lexical priming and the psychological status of collocations).

Importantly, while useful in terms of framing the discussion, wide-ranging notions such as 'formulaic language' or 'idiom principle' can also be problematic (Myles & Cordier, 2017). One important issue is the multiplicity of terms that have been employed in the literature on phraseology. For instance, in her seminal publication devoted to this topic, Wray (2002) identified as many as forty different terms that had been used in studies devoted to the formulaicity of language. Granger (2009) has rightly referred to this as a terminological chaos which besets this strand of research.

A related challenge is that the literature abounds in a wide range of definitions that encompass different types of phrases, without necessarily doing justice to how items presented as collocations across specific studies might in fact differ from each other along the key dimensions of formulaicity such as fixedness, non-compositionality, familiarity or L1–L2 congruence. A case in point is an oft-cited study by Webb et al. (2013), which examined the process of incidental learning of L2 collocations. The target items in this study included phrases of varied phraseological status (e.g., 'cut corners', 'pull strings', 'throw light'), which, in the light of the non-literal meanings of some of these phrases, could arguably be categorised as idioms rather than collocations. Such examples then show how the categorisations of specific phrases are highly dependent on individual scholars' decisions to adopt specific criteria and definitions (see Peters et al., under review, as an instance of a study which deliberately uses the term 'multiword units' as a broader category).

Commenting on such difficulties in defining and categorising examples of formulaic sequences, Wood (2020) observes that it is common for authors to hedge their claims about formulaic language and the multifaceted nature of research in this area. Similarly, Granger (2021) points out how different operationalisations and definitions found in phraseological research render it difficult to compare findings across studies, particularly if data collection involves different designs or research protocols.

Taking all of the above into account, this Element treats collocations as a category of formulaic language but underlines the importance of establishing clear and replicable definitions, with corpora treated as a useful source of insights into the graded nature of collocability. The next section specifically explains how the identification of collocations can benefit from corpus-derived information.

2.3 Defining Collocations as a Graded Phenomenon

Having introduced the wider context for this Element, it is important to say that collocation is a topic that has been attracting increasing amounts of attention in corpus linguistics and beyond. Gries (2013, p. 159) goes as far as stating that 'collocation has been, and will remain, one of the most important concepts' in corpus-based inquiry. At the same time, he also calls for careful consideration of how collocations can be defined depending on specific research purposes. Similarly, Gyllstad and Wolter (2016) observe that when one looks at published collocation research, what is referred to as a collocation varies greatly both within and across studies, which compounds the task of adopting appropriate and commonly accepted definitions.

Broadly speaking, collocations can be regarded as word partnerships, with collocation research putting a strong emphasis on different types of lexical and lexico-grammatical relations and patterns. Specifically, corpus-assisted analyses of the lexical company of individual items help to reveal new facts not only about word co-occurrence, but also recurrence, meta-phoricity, creative use of language and many more. Also, with linguistic knowledge and use viewed as a formulaic-creative continuum (Ellis et al., 2015), analyses of the collocability of words help to investigate and identify collocations as a graded phenomenon with different degrees of probability (Sinclair, 2004).

Quote 2

Sinclair et al. (2004, p. 72) 'There is no hard and fast distinction between a casual and regular collocation, simply different degrees of probability.'

For instance, such a graded view of collocations can be found in Granger's (2021) discussion of learner corpus research (for details on learner corpora, see Section 4.2). Rather than employing binary categories of collocations versus non-collocations, the author calls for approaching L2 learner production by means of a range or cline, where pairs of words may be more or less strongly associated and psycholinguistically entrenched. From this perspective then, if collocations are a graded phenomenon, the key task for individual corpus users working across different data sets is to ensure that clear and reproducible criteria are applied, leading to more consistent and comparable findings (e.g., compari-sons of collocations retrieved from corpora that represent different L2 learning and teaching contexts).

This is where Gries's (2008; 2013) work is highly relevant, because he offers a number of recommendations to be taken into account while conducting research into collocations and other phraseologisms. He approaches phraseolo-gisms in a rather broad way, defining them as 'the co-occurrence of a form or a lemma of a lexical item and one or more additional linguistic elements of various kinds which function as a semantic unit in a clause or sentence and whose frequency of occurrence is larger than expected on the basis of chance' (Gries, 2008, p. 6). Such a broad perspective is inevitable when the ambition is to encompass as many types of phraseological units as possible. Additionally, Gries also argues that we need to be mindful of several dimensions of word co-occurrence phenomena if the field is to ensure comprehensibility, comparability and replicability of findings across different studies:

The nature of the elements involved in a phraseologism
The number of elements involved in a phraseologism
The number of times an expression must be observed
The permissible distance between the elements involved
The degree of lexical and syntactic flexibility of the elements involved
The roles semantic unity and semantic non-compositionality/non-reductability
  play in the definition

As Gries (2013, p. 136) stresses, these considerations underlie 'most of the work using collocations' and therefore constitute a good starting point to adopt more rigorous definitions and improve the quality of corpus-based phraseological research. By way of example, for a corpus linguist searching collocations in a given corpus, there are a number of questions they are likely to face:

- How many words should I include or allow in my definition of a collocation? For most linguists, collocations are typically two content words as in 'power-ful car', but for phrases such as 'make a mistake', it is also important to decide how to treat articles or other grammatical elements.
- Which words classes does my definition of collocations focus on (e.g., verb–noun collocations vs. adjective–noun collocations)?
- How many times should a given collocation occur in my corpus before it can be included as a target item worth studying by an L2 learner? Put differently, what is the required minimum frequency threshold (e.g., 10 times per million words)?
- If individual elements of a collocation occur in different forms (e.g., the collocation 'make a mistake' realised as the forms 'make', 'made', 'making'), do I include all of them under the lemma [make] as my unit of analysis or do I search for each of these forms separately?
- Does my search include only contiguous (adjacent) elements or should my collocation window allow some empty slots to take into account syntactic flexibility (e.g., passive voice constructions in collocations such as 'mistakes are made')?

While highly relevant for corpus-based explorations of L2 phraseology, regret-tably most of these questions are not easy to answer, which constitutes a challenge from the research point of view. In fact, the idea of writing this Element was partly motivated by such recurring challenges related to, for instance, establishing replicable criteria in defining and identifying examples of specific collocations. What follows then is a summary of the current debate and main approaches adopted in collocation research, reflecting upon and synthesising the ever-increasing number of empirical studies investigating the notion of collocations (for a collection of collocation studies, see Barfield & Gyllstad, 2009; for a short overview specifically focused on L2 collocations, see Szudarski, 2017).

2.4 Main Traditions in Collocation Research

2.4.1 Phraseology-Based Definitions

As aptly summarised by Gyllstad and Wolter (2016, p. 297), 'different definitions of what a collocation is abound in the literature', but it is possible to discern two dominant trends or research strands: a phraseological approach and a frequency-based one. The phraseological approach is considered a more traditional school of thought; it is typically associated with Eastern European research into phraseology and employs linguistic criteria as the basis for the categorisation of phraseological units (e.g., Cowie, 1994). Specifically, this approach relies on features such as semantic transparency, restrictedness and phraseological specialism to assess the collocability, idiomaticity and connectedness of specific phrases. As Howarth (1998, p. 27) emphatically states, phraseological significance, due to its complexity, is something less tangible than any computer algorithm can reveal, implying that intuition and judgement on the part of the analyst are necessary to study relations between co-occurring words and discern the numerous ways in which they can be combined. Inevitably, since semantic transparency or restrictedness are not clear-cut criteria, such judgement of phraseological significance involves a large degree of subjectivity, giving rise to different interpretations and consequently affecting the applicability or consistency of this approach (Granger, 2021).

Howarth (1996; 1998), for instance, is one of the authors often cited as representative of this line of phraseological research. In his continuum model of phraseology, he lists the following four categories of word combinations: free combinations ('blow a trumpet'), restricted collocations ('blow a fuse'), figurative idioms ('blow your own trumpet') and pure idioms ('blow the gaff'). Thus, with respect to the fixedness of phrases for instance, this model operationalises collocations as arbitrarily restricted pairs of words, which are more fixed than free combinations but less fixed than idioms. In turn, as regards meaning decoding, collocations are seen as more transparent than non-compositional and often metaphoric idioms.

Importantly, while not devoid of subjectivity in terms of delineating between the specific types of phrases, this continuum model has been influential in inspiring collocation research, mostly because of its great descriptive value and the potential to make linguistic distinctions. A good illustration of this is Gyllstad and Wolter's (2016) study, which used Howarth's model to test the way different types of word combinations are processed by L1 and L2 users. Study Box 1 presents details of this study.

STUDY BOX 1

Gyllstad and Wolter (2016)

Background & Aims: Considering numerous ways in which words can combine with each other as phrases, there are different linguistic criteria (e.g., semantic transparency or levels of fixedness) that are used to distinguish between free combinations ('pay a bill'), collocations ('pay a visit') and idioms ('pay the piper'). The study sought to investigate the processing of such different combinations in the L1 and L2, as indicated by participants' responses to a semantic judgement task. From the perspective of corpus linguistics, it is worth stressing that the linguistic properties of all the target items were controlled for, including phrasal frequency in the Corpus of Contemporary American English (COCA), length of phrases, the number of their cognates in participants' respective languages and collocational congruency understood as L1–L2 translation equivalence of the constituent co-occurring words.

Research Question(s)

1. For advanced L2 users of English, is there a processing cost for collocations compared to free combinations in terms of reaction times and error rate values?
2. Is the pattern the same or different for L1 users?
3. Is Howarth's descriptive distinction between free combinations and collocations in the continuum model reflected in processing differences?

Methodology

- Twenty-seven L1-Swedish advanced-level users of English and thirty-eight L1-English users
- Reaction times and error rates measured in response to three types of phrases: free combinations ('kick a ball'), collocations ('draw a conclusion') and baseline items (combinations of random words)
- All target items were congruent between Swedish and English to avoid cross-linguistic influence (for a detailed discussion of congruency effects, see Wolter & Gyllstad, 2013)

Results & Discussion: For both groups of participants, processing collocations was found to be more demanding than processing free combinations, revealing that the phraseological features and status of phrases affect the way they are stored and processed in the mental lexicon. Interestingly from the corpus perspective, participants' results were also found to be affected by the frequency of the target items: the more frequent the phrases were in COCA, the easier they were to process. Such results are in line with other studies that reported clear frequency effects, which collectively shows that both L1 and L2 users are sensitive to phrasal frequency (see Conklin, 2020 for a useful summary). With phrases from different levels of formulaicity exhibiting different processing costs, Gyllstad and Wolter conclude by pointing to the continuum model as a useful way of operationalising the formulaic status of specific phrases. Further, they also stress how such phraseological insights can be applied to rate the pedagogical value and difficulty of collocations and other word combinations.

2.4.2 Frequency-Based Definitions

The research discussed so far indicates that when it comes to the learning, processing and use of L2 phraseology, there are a number of factors at play, including semantic transparency and phrasal frequency, or in the case of L2 users, also L1–L2 congruency effects. However, a clear downside to this phraseological tradition is the fuzzy criteria (e.g., the degree of semantic transparency or substitutability of co-occurring words) that are applied to determine the phraseological significance of specific units. As both Henriksen (2013) and Granger (2019) note, this inevitably results in a large degree of subjectivity in making distinctions between specific examples of phraseological units and rating their collocability status, which is problematic from a methodological point of view.

Quote 3
Granger (2019, p. 4) 'This [phraseological] work has resulted in the identification of very fine linguistic distinctions between units, which are extremely valuable but often based on criteria that involve a large element of subjectivity. In addition, excessive concern with a strict delineation of the field of phraseology results in the exclusion of potentially relevant units on the grounds that they are fully free and hence of no interest in an L2 teaching perspective.'

This is where frequency-based or statistical definitions of collocations come to the fore, representing the other dominant approach in collocation research. In this approach, corpus-derived information (e.g., frequency of collocations or measures of association between collocating words, see Section 3 for details) helps to tap into patterns of collocability and separate statistically significant collocations from random co-occurrence (Schmitt, 2010). Specifically, in analysing the distribution of words and their collocates bottom-up (based on co-occurrence data) rather than top-down (based on pre-determined phraseological criteria), the frequency-based approach makes use of corpus evidence to identify important collocational partnerships.

Thus, using quantitative information, the frequency-based method 'avoids the fuzziness of the phraseological approach' (Granger, 2021, p. 231), often highlighting word combinations that could otherwise be excluded if fixedness, compositionality or the collocability of specific words were applied as the defining criteria. In this approach then, most word combinations that meet specific frequency-based thresholds can effectively be categorised as collocations. Not only does this mean the process of identifying collocations is conducted in a more automatic and replicable way, but its outcomes are also likely to be different, revealing different types of phrases. In fact, to reflect this and highlight the implications of adopting specific methodologies in the extraction of phrases, some authors (e.g., Granger, 2019) make a terminological distinction between *restricted* collocations (identified thanks to phraseological criteria) and *statistical* collocations (retrieved by means of corpus criteria).

To illustrate how the frequency-based approach operates in practice, Figure 1 presents examples of the most frequent collocates of the adjective 'extenuating' in COCA, with 103 occurrences of the noun 'circumstances' as the top hit. The analysis takes the form of an automatic identification of relevant word pairs whose components occur in close proximity to each

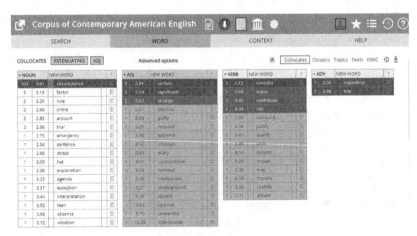

Figure 1 Most frequent collocates of 'extenuating' in COCA
(organised by part of speech)

other and whose frequencies are greater than chance. This proximity is determined with the help of corpus-based measures (see Section 3.2 for details), and a collocation window typically seen as plus or minus four words to the left and right of the search word called 'node'. Such a view of collocations stems from John Sinclair's (1991) early corpus work and its seminal impact on the field with respect to highlighting the role of collocations, idiom principle and the phraseological nature of language.

One of the main advantages of this frequency-based method is that it reflects the graded nature of collocations because, thanks to statistical information (e.g., measures of collocational proximity or strength), pairs of words found in the corpus output can be ranked or regarded as more or less tightly associated collocations. For instance, it is clear that the words 'extenuating' and 'circumstances' are tightly associated with each other, with 'circumstances' being a stronger collocate than the other nouns presented in Figure 1. That said, such an automatic identification process can also be problematic in terms of casting a wide lexical net and including different types of word partnerships, some of which – such as lexical bundles – may not necessarily form syntactically or lexically complete linguistic units typically listed in dictionaries or teaching materials (for a detailed discussion of differences between collocations and lexical bundles retrieved from learner corpora, see Granger 2019).

Referring to corpus information in such a way and treating it as an effective method for selecting relevant word pairs, many collocation studies have followed frequency-based criteria (e.g., Durrant & Schmitt, 2009; Wolter & Gyllstad, 2013; Granger & Bestgen, 2014). Study Box 2 presents Durrant and Schmitt (2009) as a study representative of this type of research.

STUDY BOX 2

Durrant and Schmitt (2009)

Background & Aims: It is argued that there are differences in the language produced by L1 and L2 users, particularly as regards the use of difficult features such as collocations. Research shows that, as language points, collocations are acquired late in the learning process and tend to pose a challenge to L2 learners, even those at advanced proficiency levels. The study then relied on corpora of academic language as a source of information with a view to exploring differences in the use of collocations by L1 and L2 writers.

Research Question(s): What are the main differences in the use of collocations in academic writing by L1 and L2 writers of English?

Methodology:
- Corpora used: a corpus of L2 academic writing (L1-Turkish and L2-Bulgarian learners) and a corpus of L1-English essays (LOCNESS Corpus); ninety-six texts in total (twenty-four long and twenty-four short texts taken from each of the corpora)
- Target collocations: adjacent premodifier–noun combinations that included adjective–noun ('green eyes') and noun–noun ('power plant') phrases
- Corpus-based criteria: frequency of collocations in the British National Corpus (BNC) and measures of their significance/strength (*t*-score and Mutual Information, MI)
- Collocations identified for each of the texts individually rather than the corpus as a whole; consequently, analysis not only in terms of text type (i.e., averages for the twenty-four texts selected in each type) but also collocational variation across individual texts

Findings & Discussion: The main finding of the study was that L2 writers resembled L1 writers with regard to the use of frequent collocations with high *t*-scores (e.g., 'good example', 'long way', 'hard work'). However, they tended to underuse strongly associated high-MI collocations, a feature that characterises the language of L1 users (e.g., 'densely populated', 'bated breath', 'preconceived notions'). While these differences were less marked in the analysis of the shorter texts, even this data pointed to similar tendencies in the underuse of specific collocations. Such results indicated then that the frequency of phrases was not the only factor that determined the learning and use of collocations in the L2; it was also the strength of association between co-occurring words, with high-MI and exclusive word combinations employed less frequently by L2 learners, suggesting that such items may require more time and exposure to be acquired in the L2.

Thus, in addition to revealing important variation in the use of collocations by L1 and L2 writers, Durrant and Schmitt's study was one of the first investigations to show the usefulness of corpus-based measures for describing different aspects of L2 collocational learning, adding methodological novelty and sparking interest in this strand of corpus research. For instance, Ellis et al. (2008) and Granger and Bestgen (2014) both adopted similar fine-grained corpus-based methodologies and demonstrated the role of both frequency and MI in analysing the use of L2 collocations.

That said, one major disadvantage associated with the frequency-based approach is that 'it lumps together units that are linguistically quite different' (Granger, 2019, p. 231). This is less than ideal for scenarios such as, for instance, selecting pedagogically valuable phraseological units that represent a specific linguistic category or may prove particularly challenging for L2 learners (e.g., collocations with delexical verbs such as 'make' or 'have'). Further, caution needs to be exercised in the application of frequency-based criteria both within and across specific corpora because, depending on what thresholds are set (e.g., minimal frequency or Mutual Information scores), the lists of collocations retrieved from different data sets can contain different items. Hence, the next section focuses on hybrid definitions of collocations, explaining how to get the best of both worlds and capitalise on combining phraseology- and frequency-based criteria for identifying important collocations.

2.4.3 Hybrid Definitions

While the two aforementioned traditions have dominated the operationalisation of collocations for research purposes, it is important to say that a hybrid approach has been gaining popularity in recent years. As the very name suggests, in hybrid definitions both frequency- and phraseology-based insights are used to delve into word collocability, co-occurrence and the ways lexical and grammatical items combine with each other, with both corpus-based and phraseological information being used to examine and classify specific phrases. In the words of Granger (2021, p. 6), the hybrid approach uses quantitative information 'to extract significant collocations in the Sinclairian sense and then to apply linguistic criteria to classify the resulting units into meaningful linguistic categories'.

Crucially, such a hybrid approach allows us to address some of the limitations identified in the two dominant approaches. As already mentioned, these are, for instance, coarsely defined boundaries and inconsistent classifications of collocations in the phraseological approach (e.g., restricted vs. idiomatic collocations). Or, to refer to the frequency-based approach at the other end of the spectrum, it may also be problematic to focus exclusively on statistical information and follow linguistically blind categorisations of recurrent phrases, without any consideration being given to their specific properties.

That is why it is not uncommon in current corpus-based research into L2 collocations to come across studies that benefit from integrating both approaches (e.g., Szudarski & Carter, 2016; Garcia-Salido & Garcia, 2018; Brezina & Fox, 2021; Boone et al., 2022). To illustrate how such a hybrid approach works in practice, Study Box 3 provides details of the latter as an example.

Study Box 3

Boone, De Wilde and Eyckmans (2022)

Background & Aims: Considering that the acquisition of L2 collocations is determined by a multiplicity of factors, the study was a learning-focused exploration of collocation development by L1-Dutch learners of L2 German. Interestingly, this development was investigated with respect to both item- and learner-related variables. The former, item-related variables, includes factors such as L1–L2 congruency, corpus frequency of collocations and association strength of their constituent elements or imageability of phrases. In turn, learner-related variables concern prior L2 vocabulary knowledge or the amount of exposure to language (L2 immersion). Boone et al.'s study is commendable in that it explored the impact of all these factors as related to the development of productive collocation knowledge, with L2 learners being tracked over an extended period of time and tested by means of a form recall test. Crucially for the present discussion, the authors adopted a hybrid definition of collocations, treating them as word combinations that represent specific syntactic patterns (e.g., adjective–noun, AN, or verb–noun, VN, collocations; see Methodology for details); these phrases also needed to occur within a given word span in a corpus and have a relatively transparent meaning (Boone et al., 2022, p. 2). Two other key aspects of the study were its longitudinal design (the same group of learners followed over a period of three years) and a focus on the learning of a language other than English. The dearth of such studies is a challenge to be addressed in future research, not only as regards collocation studies but also applied linguistics as a whole (see Section 5 for a discussion of areas that merit more attention in further research).

Methodology:
- Fifty L1-Dutch students of German at a Belgian university; the expected level of proficiency to be achieved at the end of their university education was B2/C1 of the Common European Framework of Reference

- Data collection started in year 1 (beginning of Bachelor's study) and ended in year 3 (end of study)
- Target collocations: thirteen adjective–noun phrases ('helles Bier' – 'blonde beer'), fifteen verb–noun phrases ('Stellung nehmen' – 'take position') and seven preposition–noun–verb constructions ('zu Ende gehen' – 'come to an end'); all phrases selected based on their presence in German Web Corpus 2013 and dictionaries of German collocations
- Students' collocational knowledge measured via a productive recall test; a gap-fill translation test where students provided German collocations based on L1-Dutch translations

Results & Discussion: The analysis pointed to several key findings, showing a general increase in L2 collocations, but confirming that such learning is influenced by multiple factors. First, clear L1–L2 congruency effects emerged in the data, with the presence of L1–L2 translation equivalents having a statistically positive effect on participants' learning of collocations. Interestingly, while this effect had a relatively stable influence on congruent collocations, the knowledge of incongruent items rose significantly between the data collection points. This suggests a diminishing effect of congruency over time as learners improved their collocational competence and overall L2 proficiency (see Sonbul & El-Dakhs, 2020 for similar findings). Second, the impact of corpus-based and word-related factors (frequency of collocations, their association strength and imageability) was non-significant, which contrasts with findings from studies such as Durrant (2014), where corpus frequency was one of the determinants of L2 collocation learning. Third, the analysis indicated that learners' prior productive knowledge of German vocabulary significantly predicted their collocation learning, adding evidence that 'larger vocabulary sizes, receptive or productive, are associated with better learning outcomes' (Boone et al., 2022, p. 18).

On a theoretical level, these results confirm the complex relationship between frequency effects, with L2 collocational gains likely to be mediated by a range of factors (Szudarski, 2017). Future research should establish whether such effects can be observed when, for instance, comparisons involve phrases of different levels of difficulty, or when learning takes place in more versus less input-rich environments (e.g., English as a foreign (EFL) vs. second (ESL) language). More crucially though to the present discussion, Boone et al.'s (2022) study produces several important methodological insights. Namely, it convincingly attests to the benefits of adopting hybrid definitions and studying word collocability by means of both phraseology- and corpus-based criteria. Further, by operationalising collocations from multiple angles and including a whole range of variables, Boone et al.'s design shows that L2 collocation learning can be explored with respect to both collocation- and learner-related effects. A clear advantage of this is a more nuanced and multilayered description of the incremental and complex process of L2 collocational development (see Section 3 for a discussion of different aspects of L2 collocational learning).

By way of summarising, the discussion in this section has been concerned with a range of approaches and definitions that can be adopted in collocation research, with a particular focus on contributions made by drawing on multiple criteria and triangulating sources of information. The main point to be taken is that it is essential to have a clear understanding of what is meant by a collocation in a given study and to specify what parameters are used to operationalise this construct as related to the corpus searches that are performed. This is of utmost importance in terms of methodological rigour, because not only do such parameters determine which aspects of word co-occurrence can be explored but they also have implications for the quality and depth of reported findings. As already signalled, different approaches to collocations, be it phraseology-, frequency- or hybrid-based criteria, have their own respective merits and limitations, so it is the job of the analyst to decide which definition(s) best fits their research agenda and the research questions they seek to pursue.

2.4.4 Relationship between Definitions and Identification of Collocations

In light of the reviewed research, it is clear that methodological choices are of critical importance when it comes to improving the quality of corpus-based analysis and assessing the validity of reported findings. Table 1 illustrates this point well, as it provides a variety of definitions adopted in a selection of recently published collocation studies. It also explains how the adopted criteria affected the types of phrases that were used and labelled as 'collocations'. Together with a description of the criteria and corpus measures, the discussion also highlights methodological considerations and makes recommendations for future research in this area.

None of the considerations presented in Table 1 and the challenges they pose for research are easy to overcome. Nor is it possible to say that there is necessarily only one right way of addressing such issues, because they are all interrelated and highly dependent on the research goals pursued in a given

Table 1 Examples of research studies with different criteria for defining collocations

Study	Webb et al. (2013)	Laufer & Waldman (2011)	Granger & Bestgen (2014)	Szudarski & Carter (2016)
Definition	Verb–noun collocations (semantically opaque and incongruent in terms of translational equivalence between Chinese and English, learners' L1 & L2 respectively)	Collocations as habitually occurring lexical combinations characterised by restricted co-occurrence of elements and relative transparency of meaning	Collocations defined as bigrams or directly adjacent word pairs	Adjective–noun and verb–noun collocations defined as word partnerships that frequently co-occur within a given word span and are characterised by specific degrees of fixedness
Corpora used and selection criteria	Bank of English Criteria: - t-score - collocations made up of high-frequency words (1 K most frequent word families in English)	Israeli Learner Corpus of Written English & Louvain Corpus of Native English Essays Criteria: - verb collocates of 220 most frequent nouns (these nouns occurred 20 times or more in the L1 corpus) - the same nouns were used to extract collocations from the learner corpus - collocations were considered erroneous when one of their component words	International Corpus of Learner English (ICLE); samples from L1-French, -German and -Spanish learners Criteria: - at least 5 occurrences in the BNC - automatic extraction of collocations based on part-of-speech tags: noun sequences made up of a noun pre-modified by another noun or an adjective	British National Corpus (BNC) Criteria: - a Mutual Information threshold (> 3) - fewer than 40 occurrences in the BNC - all nouns in the target collocations were infrequent words (they belonged to frequency bands outside of 3 K most frequent words in English)

Table 1 (cont.)

Study	Webb et al. (2013)	Laufer & Waldman (2011)	Granger & Bestgen (2014)	Szudarski & Carter (2016)
Examples of target collocations	*blow nose; pull strings; reach decision*	was deemed incorrect by a native speaker and was not found in the BNC and dictionaries of collocations. *get the item; inflict arguments; do a decision* (as examples of 'deviant' learner collocations)	*traffic jam; instant coffee; warm welcome*	*deep aversion; quick retort; hold a banquet*
Additional points for reflection	Some of the target phrases had both literal and metaphorical meanings (e.g., 'pull strings'), making it problematic to treat all the phrases as representing the same type of collocations. A key point to note is that such information related to the polysemy or idiomaticity of phrases cannot be identified automatically by means of corpus tools. Another important consideration is how to treat grammatical elements of collocations such as articles (a/the), whether they should be encompassed in corpus searches; note for instance that in Webb et al. (2013), 'reach decision' is presented without the indefinite article.	Considering that L2 learners may have different goals and aspirations in terms of language learning, using an L1 ('native-speaker') corpus may not necessarily be the most appropriate benchmark for assessing the quality and accuracy of their output. Further, it is important to consider where the line is drawn between correct or incorrect collocations.	In light of phraseological distinctions such as the ones proposed by Howarth (1998), it is important to decide whether phrases such as 'prime minister' or 'ladies and gentlemen' can be treated as collocations. Some linguists would categorise them as compounds and binomials, respectively.	As regards the target collocations in this study, low-frequency items were selected to ensure there was scope and room for participants' learning and lexical gains. Further, the study included both adjective–noun and verb–noun collocations. If the design had included other word classes (e.g., adverbs), participants' learning results might have been different.

| Methodological recommendations for future research | Each study needs to explicitly state what types of phrases are meant by the label 'collocations' and how that label is operationalised in research terms. If definitions of collocations are to be reproducible and replicable across studies, methodological detail is essential to improve the comparability of results. | When assessing the quality of collocations for pedagogical purposes, corpus-based criteria might need to be supplemented with pedagogical insights such as information from dictionaries and/or teachers' ratings. | In order to reliably distinguish between varied types of phrases identified across different corpora and contexts, methodological consideration and transparency in reporting are an essential part of the research process (e.g., for a useful list of criteria distinguishing between collocations and lexical bundles, see the appendix in Granger, 2019). | The selection of target items from a corpus needs to consider both the linguistic features of collocations (e.g., the word class of their constituent elements) and the overall research goals and context of a given study (e.g., in studies focused on L2 learning, a hybrid approach might be preferable). |

study. The key point however is that there are many methodological aspects to be taken into account when defining collocations, both in relation to the criteria applied as well as the kinds of claims that are made on the basis of corpus analysis and explorations of the acquisition, representation and use of L2 collocations.

Quote 4

Gablasova et al. (2017, p 171) 'Corpora, as large databases that document the products of users' word selection and co-selection, can reveal regularities in collocational preferences of users, allowing researchers to hypothesize the factors involved in the acquisition, representation, and production of these word combinations.'

2.5 Textual versus Psycholinguistic Reality of Collocations

While the focus of this Element is on collocations as a textual phenomenon studied by means of corpora, collocation research has also examined the psychological reality of word co-occurrence, exploring the extent to which different pairs of words exhibit a special psycholinguistic status. For instance, collocations can be perceived not only as frequently used lexical units, but also as associations or mental links between words known by individual L2 users (Barfield & Gyllstad, 2009; Henriksen, 2013; Durrant, 2014). From a theoretical point of view, the best exemplification of such research is Hoey's (2005) notion of lexical priming, which links corpus-based findings with psycholinguistic views on the mental lexicon. Specifically, corpus-based analyses of lexical priming are concerned with unpacking different elements of word co-selection and posit that speakers and writers are primed to use language as specific collocational configurations shaped and reinforced by their idiosyncratic language experience.

Quote 5

Hoey (2004, p. 21) 'All lexical items are primed for grammatical and collocational use, i.e., every time we encounter a lexical item it becomes loaded with the cumulative effects of these encounters, such that it is part of our knowledge of the word that it regularly co-occurs with particular other words or with particular grammatical functions.'

An exhaustive review of studies into the psycholinguistic status and representation of collocations is beyond the scope of this work, but it is sufficient to say that a number of researchers have addressed this issue (e.g., Ellis et al., 2008; Carrol & Conklin, 2020; Sonbul & El-Dakhs, 2020; Vilkaitė-Lozdienė & Conklin, 2021; Shi et al., 2023). Combining corpus and psycholinguistic methodologies, these studies have tapped into the use and processing of specific types of phrases and shown that their entrenchment in memory is dependent on frequency, fixedness, phraseological status and many other factors. Indeed, research at the interface of the textual and psycholinguistic reality of collocations clearly indicates that different types of collocational units retrieved from corpora may be independently represented in speakers' mental lexicons and in consequence exhibit different processing patterns, depending on phrases' specific linguistic properties, including their collocational status and degree of formulaicity (for a detailed discussion, see Carrol & Conklin, 2020).

Research into collocation as extended units of meaning is a good illustration of corpus-based work in this line of inquiry. As Stubbs (2009) usefully explains, work in this area follows Sinclair's phraseological view of language and focuses on notions such as semantic preference or semantic prosody. The former refers to tendencies of words to cluster together as units of language that share semantic features (e.g., the verb 'undergo' often collocating with words related to medicine such as 'surgery', 'testing', 'treatment'), while the latter is concerned with evaluative or attitudinal meanings that result from the co-occurrence of words within collocations. For instance, the verb 'cause' and its negative collocates such as 'accidents' or 'delays' is an oft-cited example of semantic prosody; see also Hunston's (2022) analysis of the semantic prosody of 'have one's cake and eat it' as related to expressing speakers' intentions. Similarly, referring to this kind of manifestation of phraseological patterning, Partington (2004) treats semantic preference and semantic prosody as distinct yet interdependent aspects of collocational meaning expressed at higher levels of abstraction. Crucially, such abstract aspects and nuanced differences in collocational meanings are rarely apparent out of context when words are viewed in isolation; rather they can only be discovered if large amounts of authentic text are grouped and analysed together, revealing yet again the pivotal role of corpora in unpacking the complex relations between words and how lexical co-occurrence affects the creation of meaning.

In closing, Section 2 has reviewed different approaches to defining collocations and presented a number of ways in which word partnerships and co-occurrence phenomena can be examined. By situating collocation studies within the ever-increasing body of corpus work into formulaic language, the discussion has outlined the main traditions in collocation research and highlighted the importance of adopting clear definitions of what is meant by the term collocations. With the caveat that corpora, while useful, are still only proxies for authentic language experience and use (Gyllstad & Wolter, 2016; Conklin, 2020), the section has also pointed to the key methodological considerations in handling and interpreting corpus data when investigating the intricate and complex learning and use of L2 collocations. Indeed, corpora do enable many ways and methods in which the frequencies and distribution of collocating words can be explored in relation to specific language users and L2 contexts. This is the focus of the next section, which addresses the main types and mechanics of corpus-based collocation analysis.

3 Types of Analysis, Measures and Dimensions in Corpus-Based Collocation Research

The aim of this section is to provide an overview of the main methods and types of analysis that are applied in corpus-based research into collocations. First, the main types of corpus analysis are presented, explaining how they draw mainly on quantitative frequency-based information but recognising also the value of qualitative insights as well. Next, the discussion focuses on the most commonly used corpus-based measures of collocations, commenting on their pros and cons and underscoring the importance of informed methodological decisions. This methodological theme is continued in the final subsection which calls for more synergy between quantitative and qualitative forms of corpus analysis and highlights the benefits of mixed-methods approaches in studying different dimensions of word co-occurrence and phraseological patterning.

3.1 Types of Corpus Analysis

Corpus linguists have a wide range of techniques and types of analysis at their disposal, including, among others, frequency analysis, collocation analysis, concordancing or keyword analysis (for a detailed discussion, see chapter 2 in Szudarski, 2018). In an overview of corpus methods employed in vocabulary studies, Durrant et al. (2022) divide the types of analysis into two broad categories: (1) quantitative (frequency-based) methods employed to study the distribution of specific linguistic features (e.g., the occurrence of the most frequent noun collocates of the verb 'take' in a general corpus of British English), and (2) qualitative methods that focus on specific uses of collocates and their meanings in a given register or discourse domain (e.g., types of adjectives that collocate with the word 'immigrant' in a corpus of British newspapers).

Examples of quantitative methods in vocabulary studies include analyses of commonly occurring phrases, proportions of word types and tokens (e.g., type–token ratios), or more sophisticated techniques such as multidimensional analyses of the distribution of specific items across texts or sections of corpora. Importantly, what all these types of analysis have in common is that they are based on frequency information quantified by means of corpus-based statistics. In turn, qualitative corpus analysis is often understood as key-word-in-context

(KWIC) analysis, where lines of text known as concordances are used to conduct a more contextualised analysis with a view to identifying specific patterns, their recurrence, discourse functions and context-specific meanings (see Section 3.4 for details).

That said, it is important to remember that much of the current corpus research skilfully combines elements of quantitative and qualitative analysis, with many areas of study and research questions benefiting from an effective and complementary integration of both types of information (O'Keeffe et al., 2007; Szudarski, 2018; Durrant et al., 2022). Collocation research is a prime example of this, in the sense of showing how valuable insights about co-occurring lexical and lexico-grammatical patterns can be drawn both quantitatively by means of statistics but also qualitatively through a more nuanced, item-based and contextualised analysis. As Durrant et al. (2022) explain, it is not only lexical collocations which can be studied with the help of corpora, but also other types of co-occurrence phenomena, including colligations understood as syntactic preferences (e.g., ditransitive constructions of the verb 'give' with direct and indirect objects) or constructions consisting of pairings of forms and meanings (e.g., 'see someone do something' vs. 'see someone doing something'). Based on these examples, it is clear that different lexical and lexico-grammatical relations between words have been subject to extensive corpus investigations, with both quantitative and qualitative methods being applied to draw useful conclusions.

Thus, the key point stemming from this discussion is that automatic searches based on frequency and statistics can be optimally accompanied by more qualitative explorations of linguistic material, including phrases and their constituent parts (both nodes as the main elements and collocates), as well as analyses of how words attract or shun each other within specific phraseological units. With this in mind, the following discussion outlines the most commonly used corpus-derived measures and statistical tests that are employed in collocation research. In order to address these matters in a concrete manner, a selection of relevant corpus-based studies is also presented, focusing on particular methodological aspects and showcasing examples of best practice that should inspire further empirical work in this area.

3.2 Corpus-Derived Measures of Collocations

One of the main aspects of corpus-based analysis of collocations is studying the frequency of nodes, that is, search words that are of interest in a given study, their collocates and the various ways in which these elements co-occur (see Figure 2 for an example search for collocates of the word 'cause'). Depending

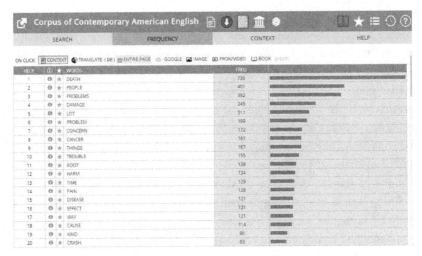

Figure 2 Most frequent noun collocates of 'cause' in spoken COCA

on one's research focus, such a collocation analysis can be carried out in a specialised corpus (e.g., the Cambridge Learner Corpus) or a large general-purpose corpus, where it is possible to check the frequency of collocates in general language use and across specific registers (e.g., the spoken subsection of COCA as in Figure 2). The main premise here is that an analyst uses a collocational window (span) within which potential word collocability can be examined. On a methodological level, most corpus linguists tend to accept the span of plus or minus four words to the left and right of the node as a large enough space to capture all relevant collocational patterns. As stressed by Gablasova et al. (2017, p. 158), when identifying examples of collocations, it is necessary to consider 'the distance between the co-occurring words and the desired compactness (proximity) of the units' (but see also Vilkaitė, 2016 and Vilkaitė & Schmitt, 2019, for interesting examples of non-adjacent collocations such as '*provide* some of the *information*').

With the frequency of use being a major variable in language learning research (Gablasova et al., 2017), the ranking of words and collocations based on their occurrence in a given corpus has proven to be a useful research method. For instance, in many collocation studies focused on L2 teaching, frequency-based rankings have been applied to decide or earmark these collocations that should be targeted through formal instruction (see Section 4 for details). However, in addition to frequency, corpus linguists interested in phraseology have also worked with a number of statistical measures which have added sophistication to the analysis and allowed to explore different dimensions of co-occurrence and for-mulaicity (see Evert, 2009 for a detailed account). Specifically, corpus-based collocation research has made use of measures that determine statistical significance (e.g., *t*-score), show the strength of association (e.g., Mutual Information or Log Dice) or tap into exclusivity between co-occurring words (e.g., Delta P). The following subsection reviews all these measures, paying particular attention to the kind of information they provide as well as providing methodological guidance to underpin high-quality collocation research.

3.2.1 T-Score and Frequency of Collocations

The *t*-score is a corpus-based test which belongs to the category of significance- and hypothesis-testing measures. It tests the level of confidence in the evidence accumulated in a given corpus in terms of the representation or distribution of word co-occurrence in language at large. Based on comparisons between the observed and expected frequencies of words, the *t*-score 'evaluates how much evidence there is that a particular combination occurs more frequently than we would expect by chance alone, given the frequencies of its component parts' (Durrant, 2014, p. 455). As such, this test has been used widely in corpus-based research (particularly in earlier studies), with the value of 2 typically treated as a minimal threshold that indicates important collocations (e.g., 'long time' or 'great deal' in Granger & Bestgen, 2014).

However, there are certain problems with the application of such thresholds, particularly when corpora of different sizes are compared with each other. As Durrant et al. (2022) explain, the *t*-score as a frequency-based measure of collocations reflects the amount of data considered in the analysis, which means it tends to be highest when there is a lot of corpus evidence (i.e., items that have many tokens in a corpus). Consequently, the *t*-score favours phrases that consist of high-frequency words, which is problematic if the analysis is to capture a whole spectrum of collocability and include word pairs from across different frequency levels. Another problem is that the *t*-score does not consider directionality within collocations; that is, it takes no account of which constituent word is the node and which is a collocate or how they may attract or shun each other in terms of collocability. Finally, there are also studies (e.g., Vilkaitė-Lozdienė & Conklin, 2021) which show that, when it comes to the identification of collocations, *t*-scores underperform compared to other corpus measures such as Delta P or MI, as *t*-scores provide little new information over what is revealed by the analysis of raw frequencies of words.

On a practical and methodological level then, when interpreting *t*-scores, caution needs to be exercised, especially with data retrieved from different corpora. It is recommended that instead of using arbitrary cut-off points to

determine whether a phrase is significant or not, *t*-scores should be employed
to rank specific items as more or less strong collocations, which better reflects
the graded nature of collocability (Durrant et al., 2022; McCallum & Durrant,
2022). Additionally, as Ellis (2012) rightly observes, it is important to
remember that even if a collocation reaches a given frequency threshold,
this does not automatically imply its pragmatic significance or psycholinguistic salience for particular speakers who represent different registers or
language domains.

Quote 6
Ellis (2012, p. 28) 'High-frequency *n*-grams occur often. But this does not
imply that they have clearly identifiable or distinctive functions or meanings;
many of them occur simply by dint of the high frequency of their component
words, often grammatical functors. The fact that a formula is above a certain
frequency threshold does not necessarily imply either psycholinguistic salience or coherence.'

Fortunately, thanks to the richness of information obtained from corpora,
ranking collocates based on their frequency is not the only way of describing
or categorising collocations. This is the reason why it is unsurprising that
recent collocation research has been increasingly relying on multiple measures of collocability such as Delta P or Log Dice; not only do they address the
limitations of previously popular measures, but are also based on more
sophisticated theoretical and computational grounds (see Section 3.2.3 for
details). Further, there are many dimensions of collocability that can be
studied by relying on a range of tests, each of them producing novel and
more nuanced information about the nature and pattens of word co-
occurrence. With this in mind, the following paragraphs outline the main
features of such corpus measures in terms of both their pros and cons, starting
with Mutual Information as a measure of collocational exclusivity and association strength.

3.2.2 Mutual Information (MI) and Exclusivity of Collocations

Mutual Information (MI) is an example of an association measure that tests the
strength, tightness and exclusivity of a relationship between two words.
Expressed as a normalised score (logarithmic scale), MI is a ratio between the
observed frequency of a given collocation and its expected frequency calculated
as the random co-occurrence of its constituent words (Gablasova et al., 2017).
Thus, MI measures the strength of the relationship between word A and word
B in terms of how much they attract each other, with corpus-based collocation
studies, particularly earlier research in this area, typically using the value of 3 as

an indicator of strong collocations (e.g., Szudarski & Carter, 2016). However, just like with *t*-scores, more current research suggests that there is little basis for applying such cut-off points, because MI should preferably be used as a gradient score, allowing to rank collocations with higher and lower levels of strength and exclusivity (McCallum & Durrant, 2022).

Further, if we accept that MI determines 'the extent to which the two words appear predominantly in each other's company' (Öksüz et al. 2021, p. 85), it can be taken as a measure of the exclusivity and uniqueness of phrases. Two important disadvantages however are that MI is a unidirectional measure in that it ignores potential asymmetry within collocations (see Section 3.2.3 for details); and it also favours lower-frequency items (e.g., it prioritises exclusive phrases or technical names used in narrower contexts, genres or language domains). For instance, Hunston (2022) discusses the technical collocation 'species mutability' found in her corpus comprising words from the book *The Rough Guide to Evolution*, with the word 'mutability' being the strongest MI-based collocate of 'species'. Similarly, Granger and Bestgen (2014) provide technical phrases such as 'nitrous oxide' or 'hippocratic oath' as examples of top-ranked collocations with highest MI scores.

In light of these examples, it can be said that in the analysis of collocations based on MI, it is not only phrasal (collocational) frequency but also word-level frequency that plays an important role. If a given word occurs rarely in a corpus, it might form strong and exclusive collocations only with a small group of specific words, and typically it is such rarer exclusive combinations that get higher MI scores (e.g., technical phrases). In short then, while MI provides useful information, being a non-directional measure and favouring low-frequency collocations, it offers only a partial or one-sided view of collocational patterning (Gablasova et al., 2017).

Considering these limitations, it is recommended that findings in collocation research should not be based on just one measure (Durrant et al., 2022; Hunston, 2022). As Deng and Liu (2022) explain, depending on the research goals and types of data at hand, a range of measures of collocational strength can supplement each other, taking into account statistical information on the one hand, and semantic and structural aspects on the other. If this is the case and several measures are considered simultaneously, the process of identifying target collocations can be greatly enhanced. Specifically, not only does this help analysts tap into the complexities and multidimensionality of the co-occurrence phenomena, but also increases the methodological rigour and sophistication of their analysis, taking into account the specificity of data, the language domains it represents and the types of phrases that are searched for.

Quote 7

Deng and Liu (2022, p. 213) 'It would seem best for researchers to select association measures based on the types of collocations and genres they are working on and perhaps combine several association measures in the identification of their given target collocations.'

3.2.3 Delta P, Directionality and Asymmetry of Collocations

Delta P is another measure that has been applied in corpus-based explorations of collocations, although to a much lesser extent than the previous two. Stefan Gries (2013; 2015) has been the main proponent of Delta P, pointing to the directionality and asymmetry of collocations (backward and forward collocations) and stressing how their constituent words may attract each other with unequal strength. To use 'extenuating circumstances' as an example, depending on which word is taken as the node ('extenuating' or 'circumstances'), the strength of the collocational attraction might be different. Specifically, if we check this collocation in a big corpus such as COCA, it turns out that there is a limited number of nouns that follow 'extenuating' as its collocates, while 'circumstances' is preceded by a wider range of options taking the form of adjectival collocates (e.g., 'certain' or 'normal'). In view of such asymmetry, it can be concluded then that the collocation between 'extenuating' and 'circumstances' is much stronger than in the opposite direction. Further, in such a directional method of collocation analysis, one collocational element may often be easier to predict on the basis of the other, because collocational attraction is not equal in both directions (Gablasova et al., 2017). The phrase 'of course' is a useful example of this, with Gries (2013) explaining how 'course' is much more restricted in its distribution as a collocate and therefore constitutes a better cue to 'of' than 'of' is to 'course'.

In this context, Delta P has been proposed as a directional measure that emphasises the probable nature of collocational pairs, with its main advantage being that it helps us 'improve the fit or understand the lack of it between corpus and psycholinguistic data in relation to associations (and their strength) between different words' (Gries, 2013, p. 153). Interestingly, there are several examples of corpus-based studies where asymmetrical backward and forward collocations have been considered. For instance, Kjellmer (1991) refers to left- and right-predictive collocations, with 'Achilles heel' and 'moot point' belonging to the latter category. Also Vilkaitė-Lozdienė and Conklin (2021) focus on such forward and backward collocations, examining whether reversed backward phrases ('attention attract') retain processing advantages typically found in the processing of canonical forward forms ('attract attention'). Interestingly, the study included examples of such collocations from both English and Lithuanian, aiming to establish whether the same processing patterns hold across typologically different languages. Results revealed that across both languages there was a clear processing advantage for forward collocations, while for backward collocations this effect was found only in Lithuanian, which syntactically, unlike English, allows a reversed order of words. Not only do these findings confirm that corpus-derived collocations become entrenched in a speaker's memory and are processed faster than non-collocations, but also that this effect holds even when phrases are presented in a reversed order, provided that such configurations are allowed grammatically in a given language. Such studies clearly indicate very close links between the patterns of co-occurring words found in corpora (textual level) and their psycholinguistic reality (psycholinguistic level) in terms of the strength and directionality of lexical associations present in the speakers' minds (recall Section 2.5 and the discussion of lexical priming as related to collocations).

In a similar vein, Malec (2010) convincingly illustrates the significance of directionality and asymmetry in analysing and testing the knowledge of L2 collocations with different levels of collocational 'headedness'. Study Box 4 presents details of this study.

Study Box 4

Malec (2010)

Background & Aims: There are many types of collocations which comprise different parts of speech (e.g., verb–noun or adjective–noun collocations) and whose constituent words represent various levels of collocational symmetry or headedness. Such headedness refers to the relative prominence of the constituent words within collocations, in the sense of their directionality and strength. For instance, in the asymmetrical collocation 'hit jackpot', 'jackpot' is the head because when the frequencies of this collocation and its constituents are analysed in a corpus, the verb 'hit' is more likely to co-occur with the noun 'jackpot' than the other way around. In other words, the attraction or linguistic association between the constituents of the phrase is stronger between 'jackpot' and 'hit' than it is between 'hit' and 'jackpot', showing the asymmetrical nature of this relation. Given the presence of such asymmetrical collocations in language at large (e.g., 'clench fist' or 'declare war'), Malec's study sought to examine the impact of such directionality as a factor affecting the difficulty of collocation knowledge and L2 learners' performance on a collocational test.

Research Question(s): Does the choice of the target word (node vs. collocate) have an impact on the difficulty of test items measuring L2 learners' knowledge of asymmetrical collocations?

Methodology
- Test of collocational knowledge administered in two rounds: one where no additional clues were provided (twenty-eight L1-Polish students of English) and another one with the first letter of missing collocations serving as prompts (fifty-two students)
- On this test, each item consisted of two sentences that conveyed the same meaning, with the target collocation missing from the second sentence; test takers needed to provide these collocations in response to prompts: either a head or a non-head of the collocation was given
- Target collocations: forty verb–noun asymmetrical collocations, selected from the BNC based on phrasal frequencies as well as the frequencies of their constituent elements; if 'hit jackpot' is taken as an example, it is found 36 times in the corpus, with 'hit' and 'jackpot' occurring 10,387 and 125 times, respectively
- In order to calculate the headedness of this collocation, its phrasal frequency was divided by the verb frequency and then multiplied by 100 (36/10,387 x 100 = 0.35%); when 'jackpot' was treated as the collocation's head or node (36/125 x 100 = 28.80%), it was found to occur in the vicinity of the verb 'hit' in almost 30% of all its occurrences; in contrast, this likelihood was much lower when 'hit' was considered the head (only 0.35% of all its occurrences were collocations with 'jackpot')
- Same procedure was used to select the remaining thirty-nine items; 'clench fist' or 'declare war' were classified as examples of verb-headed collocations, while 'pay visit' or 'lose temper' as noun-headed collocations

Findings & Discussion: Results indicated that L2 learners' recall of asymmetrical phrases was easier when the head of the collocation was present. For instance, recalling the collocation 'clench fist' was found to be easier when the head 'clench' rather than the non-head 'fist' was provided. Not only does this convincingly illustrate the significance of directionality in conducting corpus-based searches of collocations; these results also have important implications for defining and assessing collocational knowledge. It is clear that, depending on which items are used to test this knowledge, learners might find it more difficult to produce more asymmetrical or tightly associated phrases. Further, researchers also need to make an important decision whether their tests of collocational knowledge tap into the knowledge of whole collocations ('clench fist') or individual collocates ('fist'), because the format of the test is also likely to affect the difficulty and validity of such measures.

Malec (2010) is a commendable example of a study that underscores the importance of collocational asymmetry, clearly showing the need for more research along these lines. It is fair to say that much of the collocation research published to date has provided insufficient detail in this regard, often remaining silent on the directionality of lexical relations. This is largely due to the fact that most collocations studies have included unidirectional measures such as *t*-scores and MI. Encouragingly, as new corpus tools such as GraphColl (Brezina et al., 2015) or Sketch Engine (Kilgariff et al., 2014) have become available, it is now possible to include a range of measures that provide a new window into different dimensions of collocability, as well as allow visualisation of different kinds of relations between words.

By way of example, Figure 3 presents a word sketch produced via Sketch Engine, demonstrating the most frequent collocates of the word 'clench' in different positions and directions. 'Tooth', 'fist' and 'hand', for instance, are strong collocates that typically follow 'clench' as objects, while 'stomach' functions as a subject collocate. Note also that the choice of the search term (the infinitive 'clench' vs. the broader lemma which encompasses 'clenched', 'clenching', 'clench') influences what examples of collocates are identified (e.g., collocations such as 'clenched tooth' are unlikely to be identified if the

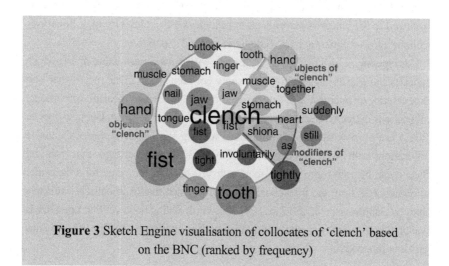

Figure 3 Sketch Engine visualisation of collocates of 'clench' based on the BNC (ranked by frequency)

infinitive form is used in the search). Collocational networks are another useful example of how the visualisation of corpus data through tools such as GraphColl allows more sophisticated and fine-grained analyses of dependencies between words, revealing 'second-order' collocations formed between the collocates of collocates (see Baker, 2016 for examples of collocational networks and shapes formed around the word 'troops' as found in a corpus of British newspapers).

Such additions and innovations are important developments not only in terms of enabling new types of analysis but also fostering interdisciplinary dialogue that produces insights at the interface of corpus linguistics, psycholinguistics and acquisition research. This interdisciplinary research also shows the complex nature of collocational knowledge and the value of drawing on multiple perspectives and methodological approaches (e.g., see Oakey, 2022 for a discussion of how research into collocations also benefits explorations of notions such as synonymy or antonymy).

3.2.4 Log Dice, Dispersion and Other Corpus-Based Measures

Log Dice is another corpus-based measure that has been proposed as a way to identify and rank collocations. In terms of practical applications, Log Dice is similar to MI because it shows the exclusivity of collocations, pointing to pairs of words whose components are strongly associated with each other. Crucially, one key advantage of Log Dice over MI is that it does not include expected frequencies of words into calculations, avoiding therefore the problem of highlighting the rare exclusivity of high-MI phrases. As explained previously, one of the main limitations of MI is that it assigns high scores to low-frequency collocations for which there is limited evidence in the corpus. Log Dice thus is preferred to MI when 'researchers aim to look at the exclusivity of collocations without a low-frequency bias' (Öksüz et al., 2021, p. 62).

Conceptually, Log Dice works as a scale with a maximum value of 14, which indicates the maximum level of exclusivity between words. This means that Log Dice is easy to interpret and can be used as a standardised measure to compare collocations extracted from corpora of different size. For instance, Gablasova et al. (2017) use phrases such as 'femme fatale' or 'zig zag' as examples of exclusive collocations with high Log Dice scores of over 13. The authors argue that with Log Dice, it can be seen more clearly than with MI 'how far the value for a particular combination is from the theoretical maximum, which marks an entirely exclusive phrase' (Gablasova et al., 2017, p. 164). It is worth adding however that Log Dice is available in Sketch Engine but not in other corpus interfaces, which partly explains why it is less popular.

Cohen's d is another measure discussed in the corpus literature (e.g., Brezina, 2018). It is a measure of dispersion used to express the evenness of distribution of a given collocation across different sections of a corpus. Gries (2013, p. 155) argues that if dispersion is absent from the analysis, 'both frequencies as well as co-occurrence information can hugely overestimate relevance as well as association strengths'. Other popular measures include tests such as chi-square or log-likelihood (LL), both of which are tests of statistical significance. They are employed not only to identify collocations but also key words, that is, words whose frequency is characteristically high or low in comparison to a reference corpus (see Gabrielatos, 2018 for an overview of metrics used in keyness analysis).

By way of example, many corpus studies have relied on LL as a basis for identifying important collocates for specific corpus data sets, with the following values used as the thresholds of statistical significance:

- Log-likelihood value of 3.84 corresponds to $p < 0.05$
- Log-likelihood value of 6.63 corresponds to $p < 0.01$
- Log-likelihood value of 10.83 corresponds to $p < 0.001$

However, these measures tended to characterise earlier corpus research, when the field's understanding of co-occurrence phenomena was less sophisticated. Considering the current state of knowledge, it is advisable that rather than relying only on tests of statistical significance (*t*-score or log-likelihood), measures of collocational strength, directionality and dispersion should be included or at least considered. By combining these metrics, collocations can be extracted in a more informed and reliable way, ensuring that the identified examples are both statistically significant and linguistically interesting. To illustrate this point through an example, Study Box 5 describes a study which involved multiple measures and sources of information about a range of factors that affect L1 and L2 collocational processing of collocations.

STUDY BOX 5

Öksüz, Brezina and Rebuschat (2021)

Background & Aims: There are a number of variables that affect the learning and processing of collocations by L1 and L2 users, with the effects of frequency being the major, although not the only, factor that has been explored in collocation research. With this in mind, Öksüz et al. examined the impact of word-level frequency (frequency of constituent words), collocation-level (phrasal) frequency and association strength on collocational processing in the L1 and L2. Crucially, collocational strength was operationalised by means of two different corpus-based measures (MI vs. Log Dice), which is of particular relevance to the discussion in this section.

Research Question(s): To what extent is there a difference between L1 and advanced level L2 speakers' sensitivity to word-level frequency information, collocation frequency information and collocational strength as measured by MI versus Log Dice when processing collocations?

Methodology
- Thirty L1-English speakers and thirty-two L1-Turkish advanced-level learners of English tested via an acceptability judgement task; participants indicated whether presented items were commonly used English phrases or not and their reaction times were recorded
- Target collocations: adjective—noun and L1–L2 congruent phrases, including 30 high-frequency (e.g., 'dark hair', with 300+ occurrences in the BNC XML corpus and Log Dice ≥ 7) and 30 low-frequency (e.g., 'vital information'; between 10 to 150 occurrences in the corpus and Log Dice between 2 and 4); non-collocational items (random combinations such as 'dirty time') constituted a baseline

Findings & Discussion: In terms of processing, results revealed that both L1 and L2 speakers reacted more quickly to the more frequent phrases and were simultaneously sensitive to both the word-level and phrase-level frequencies. Interestingly, the single-word frequency effects became weaker as the phrasal frequency increased, suggesting that for high-frequency collocations, the frequency of whole phrases takes priority over individual-word frequency effects, with both of types of information still accessible to the participants and activated during the task. Crucially for the purposes of the present discussion, it is also worth stressing that both groups of participants were similarly sensitive to the employed association measures, although a statistical model based on the Log Dice was better than the one based on MI, confirming the tendency of the latter to highlight infrequent collocations. Regardless of the way collocational strength was operationalised, there was no difference between L1 and L2 users, which brings into question claims (e.g., Wray, 2002) which suggest that L1 and L2 users are qualitatively different in terms of sensitivity to collocational information. It might be that the high proficiency of Öksüz et al.'s participants accounted for these findings; more broadly however these results suggest that L2 learners, similarly to

L1 users, are sensitive to frequency information and benefit from processing advantages that are afforded by formulaic phrases (Conklin, 2020).

Collectively, these are important results which give valuable insights into the complexity of frequency effects; they show that the impact of these effects on collocational learning can be observed in relation to both word-level and phrase-level representation, with L2 proficiency also likely to play a mediating role in this process. It can be theorised, for instance, that as L2 proficiency grows, there might be progression from less reliance on word-level frequency towards more reliance on phrase-level frequency (e.g., see Wolter & Yamashita, 2018; see also a more detailed discussion in Section 4), with corpus-derived metrics enabling us to tease apart such effects. Öksüz et al.'s study is therefore a helpful illustration that none of these findings into the multilayered dynamic nature of collocational learning processing would have been possible if the study design had relied only on a single measure based exclusively on raw frequency or association strength.

Quote 8
Öksüz et al. (2021, p. 89) 'One default association measure is unlikely to cover all purposes, no matter how popular it is.'

To recap, this section has been concerned with corpus-based measures and statistical tests that are applied to study collocations and capture the richness and multidimensionality of co-occurrence phenomena. The aim of this review has been to show that depending on which measure is used, 'the sets of collocations can differ quite dramatically' (Granger 2019, p. 231), which is of direct relevance to the validity of conclusions that are drawn, as well as the comparability of findings across individual studies. An important recommendation stemming from the reviewed findings is then to keep a critical eye on the methods and measures employed in phraseological research. Further, in light of the terminological and methodological complexity that characterises collocation research, it is also of paramount importance that the analyst fully understands how collocations are defined and operationalised by means of specific corpus-based methods, criteria and statistics (Gries, 2015; Gablasova et al., 2017; Durrant et al., 2022).

As Öksüz et al. (2021) point out, the use of multiple measures and metrics is a recommended practice, allowing us to tap into a range of aspects of lexical co-occurrence. In this context, it is encouraging to see that papers published in this area increasingly include a variety measures of collocability, exclusivity and collocational strength, although much more research is still warranted to explain some of the observed differences in the applicability of specific tests. On the whole, it is clear that no one method alone is adequate for the identification of collocations across different genres and corpus sizes (Deng & Liu, 2022), and studies such as Vilkaitė-Lozdienė & Conklin (2021) suggest also that the purported superiority of some collocation measures over others may not hold universally. Finally, the discussion in this section has also outlined how corpus-derived information should be best used to rank rather than categorise collocates in binary ways (Durrant et al., 2022), with a view to underscoring yet again the gradient nature of collocations.

Quote 9
Durrant et al. (2022, p. 48) 'A better approach is to recognise that frequency-based collocation is a gradient phenomenon; some word pairs collocate more strongly and other less strongly, and there is no clear dividing line that can neatly split combinations into groups of collocations vs. non-collocations.'

3.3 Synergy of Quantitative and Qualitative Analysis in Collocation Research

The discussion so far has positioned collocation studies predominantly in quantitative terms. However, as alluded in the introduction to this section, there is a wealth of useful information that corpus-based research can capitalise on through qualitative analysis. The aim of this final subsection therefore is to show how statistical, frequency-based studies of word partnerships can be combined or supplemented with more qualitative insights into corpus material. Such a qualitative analysis usually takes the form of concordancing, that is, careful reading of selected lines of text presented in the key-word-in-context (KWIC) format and discovering, often serendipitously, different relationships between co-occurring words, patterns and meanings (see Hunston, 2022 for an interesting discussion of serendipity in corpus research).

Quote 10
Brezina and Fox (2021, p. 173–4) 'The complexity of a phenomenon such as collocations always requires paying attention to different levels of interpretation of the results and possible alternative interpretations. When analysing collocations, we need therefore to consider both the quantitative aspects (collocation frequency and strength) and the qualitative and contextual aspects (types of collocations and the appropriateness of their use).'

By way of example, Figure 4 presents a sample of concordances for the collocation 'take place' from COCA, displayed in the KWIC format. For instance, it is interesting to analyse which words precede and form the co-text of 'take place' as found in academic language ('processes' in line 1, 'reactions' in line 2, 'trends' in line 3', 'scenario' in line 4, 'excursions' in line 8, 'analysis' in line 11, 'discussions' in line 12, 'transactions' in line 14). Further, thanks to the

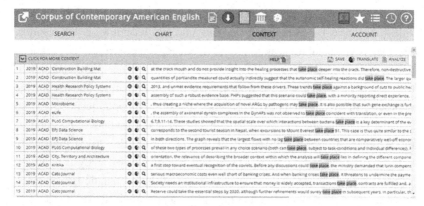

Figure 4 Sample concordance lines in KWIC format for 'take place' in COCA Corpus

KWIC format and the sorting of words it allows, the analysis can also focus on the position of these collocates, in the sense of looking at where they occur in relation to the phrase of interest (i.e., whether these collocates are immediately adjacent to 'take place' or separated by some intervening words as is the case in '*excursions to Mount Evert take place*' Finally, a qualitative analysis can also focus on frequent grammatical elements that typically precede 'take place', with, for instance, recurring examples of 'could/can take place' pointing to some interesting patterning around these modal verbs evident to the analyst even based on so few concordances. Not only are such insights valuable in terms of building a fuller collocational profile of the phrase in question, but they can also generate new research questions or trigger further searches to ascertain whether the initial observations are generalisable and hold true for other sections of the corpus.

Further examples of the importance of qualitative analyses can be found in corpus-assisted discourse studies, where an analysis of collocations serves, for instance, as a useful window into the evolution of language and the changing meanings of words over time. By way of example, see Mautner (2022) for a discussion of the changing use of the word 'leader', with its earlier (before 1980) collocates referring to 'community leader' or 'political leader', while more recently collocations such as 'team leader' or 'corporate leader' becoming more prominent. The same is true for more fine-grained corpus-based research focused on spoken language, which convincingly shows how common phrases and collocations are central to building the structure of everyday talk (e.g., see chapter 3 in O'Keeffe et al., 2007 for an insightful discussion of the pragmatic roles of phrases such as 'you know', 'I think' or 'sort of' in spoken language).

Directly relevant to this Element, the value of qualitative insights is also evident in corpus-based research into learning and teaching L2 collocations, particularly when studies seek to identify pedagogically useful or collocations or phrases that are notoriously difficult for L2 learners. A detailed discussion of these issues is provided in Section 4; here it is sufficient to underscore the importance of mixed-methods approaches that draw on both quantitative and qualitative information and use it to gain a better understanding of L2 collocation learning. A useful illustration of this is Martinez's (2013) practically oriented investigation that capitalises on both a corpus-based analysis of phrase frequencies and a more qualitative assessment of their semantic transparency and difficulty, with the overall aim of identifying pedagogically valid examples of collocations. Study Box 6 provides a summary of this study.

STUDY BOX 6

Martinez (2013)

Background & Aims: As discussed throughout this Element, there are many features which help to define collocations. For example, while frequency can be regarded as a more objective (corpus-based) criterion for identifying co-occurring words, phraseological aspects such as compositionality or learnability of phrases are more difficult to quantify in purely numerical terms and consequently may require some form of judgement on the part of the analyst. This is where a qualitative analysis of collocations proves necessary and helps to rate and select specific phrases, depending on the dimensions of collocability and formulaicity that are studied and the research or teaching goals that are pursued. Martinez (2013) is a perfect illustration of this, with his frequency–transparency framework showing how corpus-derived frequency data and a qualitative analysis of the transparency and learnability of collocations can be usefully integrated to identify and prioritise pedagogically relevant examples of L2 phrases.

Research Question(s): How can two features of multi-word expressions – frequency and semantic transparency – be used to develop a model for the inclusion of such expressions in language teaching?

Methodology
- Frequency–transparency framework (FTF) proposed as a basis for selection of pedagogically important collocations; frequency and semantic transparency of specific phrases treated as criteria closely linked to their difficulty and learnability of specific phrases in L2 contexts

- Both criteria considered more like continua rather than fixed thresholds; specifically, the arbitrary number of 500 occurrences in the BNC is used as a cut-off point between frequent ('take place') and infrequent phrases ('take credit'), while the analysis of transparency is more a matter of degree than of clear-cut categories (e.g., distinguishing between apparently more opaque ('take place') vs. more transparent items ('take credit') is largely context-dependent)
- Given that such aspects of word collocability are subject to qualitative analysis, FTF also involves L2 teachers' subjective and context-specific rating or appraisal of the pedagogical status of phrases; it is on such basis then that certain phrases can be rated as more difficult or 'deceptively transparent', that is, prone to misinterpretation by language learners (e.g., 'take issue' arguably being more difficult than 'take credit')

Findings & Discussion: Using the FTF framework, Martinez proposes the following order when it comes to ranking L2 collocations for teaching purposes: more frequent and more opaque collocations (e.g., 'take place') should be prioritised over infrequent and transparent phrases (e.g., 'take credit'). In turn, if two different phrases represent roughly the same level of frequency, the more opaque one should be selected or targeted first in L2 teaching, because it is likely to cause more difficulty or be misunderstood by L2 learners (e.g., 'take charge'). If a collocation is both infrequent and transparent, the framework suggests that such a collocation may not merit explicit pedagogical attention, with valuable classroom time being devoted instead to teaching more relevant phrases.

It is evident that this approach to collocations is very different from a purely statistical extraction as outlined in Section 2. With such automatic measures carrying the risk of being blind to some linguistic features of phrases such as transparency, what becomes equally if not more relevant in pedagogical settings are qualitative insights which 'can be crucial for getting a clearer picture of collocational patterns associated with certain groups of speakers or a certain type of word co-selection' (Gablasova et al. 2017, p. 173). Importantly, from a methodological point of view, Martinez is clear about the potentially subjective nature of such qualitative choices. In fact, he welcomes them and argues that 'what the FTF adds is a research-informed conceptual aid to help justify even intuitive decisions' (Martinez, 2013, p. 190). He is also explicit about the pedagogical rationale and applications for his framework: it is a guide rather than a universal solution, with teachers and language practitioners needing to consider many other contextual factors as well. These are, for instance, learners' proficiency or the specifics of a learning situation, factors which should also determine the selection of collocations with particular groups of learners or pedagogical purposes in mind.

To conclude, this section has focused on qualitative strands of collocation research, arguing how this type of corpus-based analysis is more nuanced and context-dependent than the purely statistical and frequency-based approaches discussed previously. It has shown that if research focus is on specific uses of collocations, their pragmatic or pedagogical functions as related to specific communicative situations, qualitative observations are valuable or even essential in some corpus-informed projects. Of course, not all research questions pertaining to collocation learning are equally amenable to such explorations. But it is important to remember that if the potential of corpus-based collocation analysis is to be fully realised, qualitative forms of analysis have much to offer in terms of describing collocations in a comprehensive, context-appropriate and ecologically valid manner. This clearly shows that corpus linguists have a whole range of methods and options at their disposal, enabling them to delve into word co-occurrence phenomena from multiple angles.

4 Corpus-Based Research into Learning and Teaching L2 Collocations

This section focuses on corpus-based research into learning L2 collocations as represented by studies lying at the intersection of corpus linguistics, second language acquisition (SLA) and language pedagogy. Aiming specifically to demonstrate the contributions of corpora in this strand of work, the discussion first refers to usage-based approaches as the theoretical basis underpinning the current explorations of L2 learning and use. Next, attention is turned to learner corpora which are presented as a source of insights into L2 collocation learning and lexical development. Topics that are addressed include the mechanics of the contrastive interlanguage analysis and applications of corpora in assessing the collocational accuracy and sophistication of L2 learner production. Finally, the last subsection discusses the implications of corpus-based research into collocations for L2 teaching and pedagogy.

4.1 Corpora, Collocations and Usage-Based Approaches to Language Learning

As stressed throughout the Element, in the last twenty to thirty years, there has been an ever-increasing amount of interdisciplinary work focused on collocations and phraseological patterning, not only from the perspective of corpus linguistics but also psycholinguistics, cognitive linguistics and SLA. As regards the latter, collocations have been studied as an important aspect of the acquisition process, particularly in relation to the development of L2 knowledge at different levels of competence. For instance, corpora have usefully shown variation in the use of word combinations by specific groups of speakers across contexts and learning settings, helping to account for differences between L1 and L2 learning and shedding new light on the features of learner language regarded as a system in its own right rather than a deficient version of L1 use (see Section 4.2 for details).

In terms of theory, much of this corpus-based work into collocations has been influenced by usage-based approaches to language acquisition. In simplest terms, these approaches emphasise language experience itself as the main source of linguistic knowledge. In usage-based approaches, language knowledge equals language use (Pérez-Paredes et al., 2020), with the experience of individual speakers playing 'an important role in the creation, entrenchment, and processing of linguistic patterns' (Conklin, 2020, p. 174). Language learning then takes the form of statistical learning, where speakers tally linguistic information from all their social encounters and build their linguistic repertoires based on exposure to input. Further, frequency effects are seen as the key mechanism that helps to explain information storage and processing by language users, showing how words, phrases and other linguistic features are entrenched and strengthened in memory (see Ellis, 2002 for detailed discussion).

It is in this context that the role of collocations becomes a central aspect because, in usage-based approaches, multi-word sequences, similarly to words, constitute the integral element of the structure of language. Although it is beyond the scope of this Element to review research into children's comprehension and production of formulaic language (see Wray, 2002 for a seminal publication, including examples pertaining to L1 acquisition), it is noteworthy that phrases are a central aspect of language learning for both children and adult learners, with lexico-grammatical units of varied degrees of complexity and abstraction forming a continuum of constructions (Pérez-Paredes et al., 2020). From heavily entrenched units such as idioms or fixed collocations (e.g., 'take issue with') to syntactically connected strings such as prepositional phrases (e.g., 'take part in'), the notion of formulaic sequences has enabled us to view language as a formulaic–creative continuum (Ellis, 2012; Ellis et al., 2015).

This is where usage-based approaches and corpus linguistics coincide because, as discussed in Section 1, corpus-based analyses have been transformational in revealing the role of collocations and phraseological units with different degrees of formulaicity as the building blocks of language. Given the focus of this Element on collocations and L2 learning, there are several key points that will be addressed next: firstly, how corpora, particularly learner corpora, have been helpful in studying collocations as a token of L2 proficiency; secondly, how corpus-based research has enabled exploration of different aspects of L2 collocational learning; and finally, the relationship between collocations and the assessment of lexical richness and sophistication in L2 texts. All of these issues are discussed in Section 4.2, with selected studies illustrating the contributions of learner corpus research (LCR) to collocation studies, the description of learner language and the broad field of SLA.

4.2 Learner Corpora, Interlanguage and SLA

Learner corpora are typically defined as computerised databases of language produced by foreign or L2 learners (Granger, 2012); as such, they provide a useful tool for investigating a wide range of issues pertinent to SLA theory and practice (for comprehensive overviews of learner corpus research, see Granger et al., 2015 or Le Bruyn & Paquot, 2021). Such corpora allow us to conduct more refined searches of learner language (Cobb & Horst, 2015) and thanks to automated analyses, it is possible to produce better data-informed descriptions of L2 competence at multiple levels of language structure, including not only lexis but also grammar, discourse and others (see Lu, 2022 for a discussion of the research intersection between corpus linguistics and SLA).

> **Quote 11**
> Cobb and Horst (2015, p. 205) 'Important among the strengths of lexically focused learner corpus research is its emphasis on investigating learner production systematically, in a way that goes beyond what can be simply observed. It pulls out patterns in learner productions, in the manner of other corpus research, but then often goes on to link these to other empirical research findings. The portrait is potentially rich and comprehensive.'

In the context of LCR and L2 studies, corpora have been particularly helpful in providing insights into the structure of interlanguage as a separate linguistic system developed by L2 users during subsequent stages of learning. When discussing LCR, Cobb and Horst (2015) specifically state that corpus-based comparisons enable us to assess the impact of L2 learners' age, proficiency level, task conditions and cross-linguistic influence on their use of words and collocations. All of these variables are of importance to language learning theory and practice, including what is highly relevant to the current discussion, the impact of such factors on the learning of collocations.

Further, due to their size and preoccupation with naturally occurring language, learner corpora have been immensely helpful in demonstrating variability in SLA, not only in terms of supporting theoretical claims but also in gaining a better understanding of how L2 learning is dependent on a whole range of factors. For instance, in relation to collocations, one of the key questions examined in this line of research has been the impact of learners' mother tongue on L2 learning and the degree to which collocation use can reflect growth in L2 proficiency. Variability in language learning is a central concept and hence a great deal of L2 research seeks to 'explain systematic differences in L2 acquisition by different (groups of) learners', recognising the role of linguistic, cultural, social and psychological determinants of the learning process (Gablasova, 2021, p. 358). Many of these issues are outlined in the following four subsections, delving into the key aspects of LCR as related to collocational learning.

4.2.1 Learner-Corpus Research and Collocations as a Token of L2 Proficiency

With reference to lexis, learner corpora have been instrumental in demonstrating links between increased L2 proficiency levels and the use of formulaic language (Paquot & Granger, 2012). Put differently, L2 learners' use of collocations and other phrases has been found to be an effective way of tracking their linguistic development, with collocational competence and the presence (or absence) of phrases affecting the way L2 output is perceived and assessed by others (e.g., Boers et al., 2006; Crossley et al., 2015; Saito, 2020). Importantly, while early SLA research paid attention to the importance of formulaic units in developing different aspects of proficiency (e.g., Peters, 1983), it was through the advent of corpora that collocations and lexico-grammatical partnerships have come to the fore of LCR, highlighting the central role of phrases in L2 learning and teaching (see Section 4.3 for details on the use of corpora in L2 teaching).

Specifically, what corpus linguistics has added to the discussion is that collocational competence can be treated as a token of L2 proficiency as learners develop linguistically and progress towards higher levels (Paquot & Granger, 2012; Paquot, 2019; Granger, 2021). In other words, a good command of collocations has come to be seen as an important proxy for L2 proficiency and fluency. To refer to the seminal publication by Pawley and Syder (1983), formulaic sequences became markers of nativelike selection and nativelike fluency and began to be treated as characteristic of successful, fluent and context-appropriate language use, although a caveat needs to be added that the term 'nativelike' is not without its problems.

Namely, in much of corpus-based studies into the role of collocations in achieving L2 proficiency, this topic has been approached by referring to notions such as 'nativelike competence' or 'nativelike use' of grammar or vocabulary. While convenient and helpful in terms of delineating differences between L1 and L2 learning, terms such as 'nativelike' or 'nativelikeness' clearly run the risk of engendering specific assumptions or expectations about L2 learning. For instance, the use of such labels creates an impression that a 'nativelike' performance, or at least striving to emulate the norms of L1 use, constitutes the ultimate goal for all L2 learners, which does not necessarily hold true across different L2 contexts and domains. In addition to the fact that there are a number of benchmarks that can be adopted in corpus-based research (Gilquin, 2022), there is substantial variation in L2 learners' linguistic needs and preferences. This includes their inclinations for collocations and phrasal vocabulary (Wray, 2019) and is particularly true for users of English as a lingua franca (see Jenkins & Leung, 2019 for a recent summary). In view of the growing body of work in this area, and this includes corpus-based work (e.g., Pitzl, 2018), it is clear that decisions about how to study and assess L2 collocation need to go beyond simple dichotomies of native versus non-native use.

Considering the aforementioned, in this Element the term 'target-like' (Lardiere, 2013) is deemed more appropriate and preferred to 'nativelike', because while the latter is used to describe L2 performance at specific proficiency thresholds, it is not devoid of vagueness that comes with the label 'native speaker'. Even more importantly, the adjective 'target-like' aims to avoid or at least reduce the ideological burden associated with the notion of nativelike performance. Consequently, while a lot of corpus studies refer to native corpora or nativelike language use as benchmarks, in the present discussion terms 'L1' and 'L2' corpora are used in order to stress the point that learner language can and should be studied as an object in its own right, without L1 performance necessarily being treated as the default position. Specifically, in what follows, the juxtaposition of L1 and L2 corpora is regarded as an important source of insights into the development of L2 competence, without necessarily portraying learner language as inadequate or insufficient in comparison to L1 use and consequently avoiding the characterisation of L2 learners as 'simply people who get things wrong' (Hunston, 2022, p. 156).

4.2.2 Aspects of L2 Collocational Learning

In the discussion of the applications of corpus methods, Durrant et al. (2022) point to a number of ways in which corpora can benefit lexical research. There are for instance studies into variation in the use of vocabulary across modes and registers (e.g., differences between spoken and written vocabulary, the occurrence of common phrases in general vs. academic English, discipline-related lexical variation) or tracking the use of collocations by L1 users (e.g., see Durrant & Brenchley, 2022 for an example study showing the development and use of L1 academic collocations).

All these types of analysis are pertinent to learner corpora as well, with a whole range of possibilities they create for exploring different aspects of L2 phraseology, including collocation learning. A useful set of parameters for studying this process has been proposed by Schmitt (2010), who explains how the acquisition of phraseological units in the L2 can be explored by referring to the following dimensions:

- Amount of use
- Accuracy and appropriacy of use
- Effectiveness and automaticity of language intuitions

Each of these could be addressed at length in its own right, not only with respect to the mechanics of corpus analysis itself but also the implications of this research for L2 teaching and pedagogy. Within the scope of this Element though, a brief discussion follows, outlining the main aspects and considering in particular how LCR has led to richer descriptions of the acquisition of collocations by L2 learners.

When it comes to the first dimension, the amount of formulaic language used by L2 learners, there is a sizeable body of corpus-based literature exploring learner production in terms of under- and overuse of collocations, typically based on comparisons between L1 and L2 corpora. An example study in this strand is Durrant and Schmitt (2009), which was already described in Section 2 and revealed L2 writers' underuse of specific collocations compared to L1 writers. Specifically, the L2 writing was characterised by fewer examples of high-MI and tightly associated pairs of words (e.g., 'densely populated'), suggesting that this type of collocations, and by extension MI as a measure of collocational strength, can be used to distinguish between L1 and L2 use.

Similar conclusions were drawn by Ellis et al. (2008), who also reported differential effects of frequency and MI as determinants of collocation competence in L1 and L2 users. While MI scores were a better predictor of collocational processing for L1 users, L2 users were more sensitive to the frequency of target phrases rather than collocation strength. Such results not only have important methodological implications (see discussion Section 2.3), but also provide useful theoretical information on L2 learning. For instance, if L2 proficiency growth is characterised by a discernible change in the types of collocations produced by learners (e.g., an increase of strongly associated, high-MI collocations or a decrease of high-frequency phrases composed of common words), then teaching materials used in the classroom or tests that seek to operationalise L2 proficiency need to pay more attention to phrasal vocabulary as an essential component of linguistic competence. Indeed, there is a growing body of corpus-based work (e.g., Crossley et al., 2015; Paquot, 2018) clearly showing that collocational accuracy plays a key role in the perception and rating of L2 learner output (see Section 4.2.4).

The second dimension of corpus-based research into formulaic language has focused on the accuracy and appropriacy of L2 collocations, with many studies examining the types of errors found in learner output contrasted with the production of L1 users. Nesselhauf (2003) produced a seminal study which sparked a great deal of interest and contributed to a better understanding of L2 collocational development. Using a corpus of essays written by L1-German of English, the study found that L2 output was characterised by erroneous or nonstandard collocations (e.g., 'make homework' rather than 'do homework', or 'take task' rather than 'carry out/perform'). Further, the study also revealed that many of these examples were traced back to the influence of learners' L1, pointing to the importance of L1–L2 congruency effects. Similar findings were reported in subsequent studies (e.g., Laufer & Waldman, 2011; Wolter & Gyllstad, 2013), suggesting that L1 transfer plays a major role in the learning and use of collocations, with L1–L2 incongruent phrases (those without direct translational equivalent between learners' respective languages) posing more learning difficulty even for advanced-level learners (e.g., Szudarski & Conklin, 2014).

With many studies in LRC centring on the accuracy of L2 collocation production (see Paquot & Granger, 2012 and Granger, 2019 for useful summaries), it is also important to mention the notion of 'phrasal teddy bears' (Ellis, 2012). While some types of phrases may be used less frequently (e.g., collocations with high MI scores) because learners 'do not know them as well and are not confident in their use' (Schmitt, 2010, p. 143), other phraseological units are found to be overused as they function as L2 learners' 'safe bets' (e.g., frequent discourse markers that are overused). This point is stressed in Wray's (2019, p. 263) recent discussion of the reasons for the apparent lack of formulaicity in learner language when compared to L1 output. Wray posits that L2 learners' overuse of favourite collocations may indicate that they are satisfied with the broad meanings and functions expressed by means of a small set of familiar and high-frequency items (collocational 'teddy bears'), which in consequence results in a less rich or varied repertoire of formulaicity. Equally, the overuse of specific collocations may also be driven by compensation strategies employed by L2 users (e.g., avoidance); for instance, when they function in intercultural contexts and wish to portray specific or multiple identities through their use of English as a global language (Kecskes, 2019). Not only do these findings inform theoretical descriptions of L2 collocation competence, but they are also relevant pedagogically and help teachers and materials writers select phrases to be targeted through explicit L2 teaching (see Section 4.3 for corpus-based research into pedagogical lists of phraseology).

The final dimension of corpus-based research into formulaic language are studies into the accuracy and automaticity of collocational intuitions by L1 and L2 users. Intuitions have been examined mostly in relation to the frequency of specific words and, to a lesser extent, collocations as well (Schmitt, 2010). From the extant research (e.g., Siyanova-Chanturia & Spina, 2015; Fioravanti et al., 2021), it appears that L2 users can develop some intuitions about the collocability of words, but this is largely dependent on the frequency and functions of specific phrases, with more frequent items generally being easier to judge or evaluate. Interestingly, this strand of corpus research is usefully complemented with insights from psycholinguistic and experimental classroom-based studies. A case in point is Pellicer-Sanchez et al.'s (2022) innovative study that delved into L1 and L2 speakers' levels of confidence about newly developed collocational knowledge. By combining traditional pen-and-paper tests with psycholinguistic measures, the study showed that learners felt more confident when their answers on a collocational test were correct, demonstrating that this dimension of collocational knowledge might indicate L2 users' readiness to employ specific phrases. Similarly, Fioravanti et al. (2021) also tapped into L1 and L2 users' perceptions of L1 and L2 users with respect to the lexical fixedness and compositionality of Italian phrases, including collocations. Results revealed that L1 but not L2 users were able to distinguish between perfectly grammatical and non-targetlike items, with collocations posing particular difficulties for the latter. As a sidenote, studies that delve into the use of collocations in languages other than English are a welcome addition, particularly when they integrate findings from across diverse research angles within language studies.

4.2.3 Contrastive Interlanguage Analysis

A key aspect of LCR research worth discussing is the contrastive interlanguage analysis or CIA (Granger, 1996; 2012; 2015), whose main aim is the exploration of learner language by analysing texts written by learners from different populations of L2 learners. As Granger (2012, p. 18) observes, some corpus analyses 'have focused exclusively on misuse and have led to the revival of error analysis in the form of computer-aided error analysis', but many studies employ CIA to compare different varieties of the same language. For instance, these could be comparisons of L2 output produced by learners from a range of L1 backgrounds or comparisons between learner varieties and L1 (expert) varieties. The former type of analysis examines the use of collocations in relation to broader SLA issues such as developmental sequences or the role of L2 proficiency, while the latter makes it possible to 'uncover typical features of interlanguage, not only errors, but also instances of under- and over-representation of words, phrases and structures' (Granger, 2012, p. 18). Study Box 7 outlines Altenberg and Granger's (2001) study as an illustration of such research.

STUDY BOX 7

Altenberg and Granger (2001)

Background & Aims: High-frequency verbs such as 'make', 'give' or 'take' have many features which make them an interesting object of study in relation to topics such as polysemy, cross-linguistic comparisons or L1–L2 translation. From the perspective of L2 learning, what these verbs have in common is that they tend to be problematic for language learners, particularly when they form collocations where verbs become delexical (e.g., phrases such as 'make a distinction' or 'make a reform', where most of the meaning is carried by the noun while the verb is arbitrarily restricted to 'make' rather than other verbs). With this in mind, Altenberg and Granger sought to examine the verb 'make' and its collocational patterning as represented by a corpus of L2 essays written by L1-French and L1-Swedish learners of English.

Research Question(s)
1. Do L1-French and -Swedish learners of English tend to over- or underuse the verb 'make' and its collocates in a corpus of L2 writing compared to L1 writing?
2. What role does the L1 play in the use of such collocations?

Methodology
- Corpora used: L1-French and L1-Swedish subcorpora of International Corpus of Learner English and Louvain Corpus of Native English Essays (c. 170,000 words each)
- Each learner essay approximately 600 words long, covering a variety of topics (argumentative and non-technical writing)

- Collocation analysis based on lemmas, a lexical unit that encompasses all inflectional forms of 'make' ('makes', 'made', 'making)

Findings & Discussion: In terms of the raw frequency of the lemma 'make', the French learners were found to underuse this verb, while the Swedish learners performed similarly to L1 users. Interestingly, as regards the use of collocations, it was the frequency of delexical phrases that led to significant differences between L1 and L2 writers. In other words, such delexical collocations were significantly underused by L2 writers, indicating their difficulty and slower progress in the acquisition and use of such phraseology. The results showed an overuse of 'make' as a commonly occurring verb but also its underuse when it was a part of collocations. Further, many collocations in the learner corpora were misused, with the delexical category accounting for the majority of errors (e.g., 'make a balance', 'making harm'). Other types of phrases with 'make' also proved difficult (e.g., 'make something possible') but only for the French writers. It is worth stressing that even though participants in this study represented high levels of English proficiency (university-level students of English), the production of correct collocations still posed challenges, which resembles the corpus-based results of Nesselhauf (2003) or Laufer and Waldman (2011). Collectively, this attests to the difficulty in acquiring such collocations by high-level L2 learners that come from diverse L1 backgrounds. It also suggests that, while the negative impact of the L1 is a major factor in collocational learning, other factors need to be considered as well (e.g., the internal difficulty of specific collocations, learners' context of learning or the amount of time devoted to teaching collocations, to name just a few).

Based on these findings, it is clear that corpus-based analyses of learner language can greatly enrich our understanding of the learning and use of phraseology in the L2. When it comes to collocations, Granger (2019) notes that there are several key findings that transpire from this growing body of empirical work:

- L2 learners use a large number of collocations and lexical bundles; much of L2 output is target-like but is also characterised by a small number of high-frequency lexical teddy bears. These are phrases that L2 users feel comfortable with and tend to cling to.
- L1 transfer is a major factor in the acquisition and use of L2 phraseology (see Section 4.3 for details).

- Amount and quality of collocations and lexical bundles develop with proficiency, with an increase in association between co-occurring words being a particularly useful measure. This means that phraseological competence can be considered an important marker or sign of L2 development.

Quote 12

Granger (2019, p. 240) 'As regards collocations, the use of quantitative methods has made it possible to go beyond traditional dichotomies, such as the sharp division between collocations and free combinations, or between correct and incorrect collocations. These dichotomies often rely on fuzzy intuition-based criteria, which are both complex to implement and difficult to replicate.'

Testament to how quickly this research is progressing is a recent volume edited by Granger (2021), which showcases the multiplicity of perspectives from which L2 phraseology can be approached. This includes L2 collocation studies such as for instance Omidian et al.'s (2021) investigation of L1-Chinese learners' writing in L2 Italian. The study provides evidence for the vital role of longitudinal corpora in analysing samples of learner language produced over longer periods of time rather than data collected at fixed points as is the case in cross-sectional studies. Such longitudinal research allows us to tap into the dynamic processes involved in the development of L2 phraseo-logical knowledge (see also Siyanova-Chanturia & Spina, 2020), showing a clear need for increasing the availability of such longitudinal corpora of learner language.

By way of summary, the research reviewed in this subsection clearly demon-strates that the agendas of LCR and SLA are highly complementary (Granger 2021, p. 12). It exhibits not only the value and potential of CIA, but also provides a good answer to criticisms levelled at corpus-based comparisons by showing that the analysis of L2 learner production can go beyond the L1–L2 comparative fallacy (Bley-Vroman, 1983). With learner corpora situated at the crossroads of corpus linguistics and SLA, corpus-based L1–L2 comparisons not only service L2 learning theory but are also 'extremely powerful heuristic techniques which bring to light hitherto undetected lexical, grammatical, and discourse features of learner language' (Granger, 2012, pp. 20–1). Also, with many new types of corpora currently being available online (e.g., Sketch Engine or the www.English-corpora.com interface; see Fernandez & Davis, 2021 for a comprehensive overview), LCR does not need to limit itself to comparisons with L1 norms. Further, studies into learner language can also draw on findings from experimental and classroom-based research (Gilquin, 2021), particularly with an increasingly important focus on triangulation efforts. Indeed, corpora have much to offer in terms of enhancing interdisciplinary collocation studies and show how L2 research can benefit from simultaneous and complementary attention to corpus linguistics, psycholinguistics and SLA.

4.2.4 Collocations and the Assessment of L2 Lexical Richness and Sophistication

LCR studies, and the analysis of L2 learners' collocational competence specifically, have also been conducted in relation to lexical richness and sophistication. As a theoretical construct, lexical richness is rather difficult to define (see Leńko-Szymańska, 2020 for details), because it encompasses different dimensions of lexical knowledge such as lexical density (the proportion of content vs. function words) or lexical diversity (defined as the ration between types and tokens in a text or corpus). With respect to corpus analysis, there are a number of measures which help to operationalise the lexical quality and richness of learner language (Cobb & Horst, 2015). For instance, lexical profilers such as Cobb's VocabProfile can produce corpus-based descriptions of L2 learner output presented as of 1,000-word bands of vocabulary identified on the basis of their frequency in a reference corpus (e.g., the BNC or COCA). In terms of collocations, L2 learners' lexical richness can be presented as the proportion of low-frequency or strongly associated phrases, the presence of which was reported to distinguish between higher- and lower-proficiency students (e.g., Granger & Bestgen, 2014). This means that corpus-based measures of lexical and collocational richness can assist the assessment of L2 output, with different indices of vocabulary influencing raters' judgement of the quality of learner language across proficiency levels (for examples, see the discussion of the English Profile).

While still in its early days, this line of corpus-based research into L2 collocational sophistication is on the increase. As Kyle (2020) explains, there is an emerging body of work investigating the notion of phraseological sophistication studied in relation to factors such as dispersion of phrases, their contextual distinctiveness (i.e., the number of contexts in which a given phrase occurs) or, crucially, the presence and quality of collocations. All of these factors are pertinent to the assessment and modelling of L2 lexical development, but given the focus of this Element, the use of collocations, is particularly relevant to the current discussion.

Paquot (2018; 2019) is at the forefront of this research, with her studies serving as examples of how indices of phraseological sophistication can be applied to assess the quality of L2 learner production. Apart from the distribution of individual words found in L2 writing (and speech, to a lesser extent), L2 lexical proficiency has also been studied by means of corpus-based indicators of collocational sophistication, including the frequency of occurrence, collocational strength (MI scores) and types of grammatical dependencies between co-occurring words (e.g., adjective–noun vs. verb–object collocations). Study Box 8 presents details of Paquot's (2018) study which is concerned with many of these issues.

STUDY BOX 8

Paquot (2018)

Background & Aims: The study aimed at examining the role of phraseological sophistication in affecting raters' judgement of L2 academic writing at three levels of English proficiency (B2, C1 and C2 of the Common European Framework of Reference for Languages, CEFR). The writing of EFL learners (students of modern languages at university level) was taken as the basis of the analysis, with phraseological sophistication conceptualised as the use of statistical collocations. These included the following types: adjective–noun phrases ('blue dress'), adverbial modifier–verb phrases ('less quickly') and verb–object phrases ('watch TV'). With the focus being the effects of phraseological sophistication, L2 writing proficiency was measured automatically by a range of indices tapping into a range of syntactic and lexical features found in the learner essays.

Research Question(s)
1. To what extent does phraseological complexity, a missing component in the CEFR, influence human raters' overall judgement of writing quality in university assignments produced by EFL learners?
2. To what extent do syntactic complexity and lexical complexity influence human raters' overall judgement of writing quality in university assignments produced by EFL learners?

Methodology
- Corpus used: Varieties of English for Specific Purposes (VESPA) learner corpus (330,000 words written by L1-French university-level students) and L2 Research Corpus (66 million words taken from published journal articles); both corpora matched in terms of register (academic writing) and discipline (linguistics)
- Analysis of the use of collocations treated as an indicator of L2 writing proficiency; corpus-based measures, including MI scores, used to

identify three types of collocations (adjective–noun, adverbial modifier–verb and verb–object relations) across samples of L2 writing at three proficiency levels (B2, C1 and C2 of CEFR)

Findings & Discussion: Unlike syntactic and lexical sophistication, phraseological sophistication was found to influence raters' judgement of L2 writing, reliably distinguishing between the B2 and C2 levels of proficiency. More specifically, higher proficiency scores were awarded to L2 texts that contained more collocations with medium to high MI scores and fewer collocations with low MI scores. Interestingly, in a follow-up study, Paquot (2019) confirmed the role of phraseology in affecting the rating of L2 writing, showing that adjective–noun collocations significantly distinguished between the B2 and C2 proficiency levels, while adverb collocations reliably distinguished between B2 and C1 and C2 levels, but not between C1 and C2 levels. Replicating these findings further and generalising beyond English, similar results were also reported for L2-Dutch texts (Rubin et al., 2021).

Such findings lie at the heart of LCR research and demonstrate how corpus-based indices help to unpack various types of relationships between words and how their presence in learner production impacts on the assessment of L2 writing. In addition to expanding methodologies for the operationalisation of phraseological sophistication, this research also makes important theoretical contributions, showing how collocational and phraseological competence ought to feature more prominently in L2 testing rubrics and descriptions of L2 proficiency.

Another prime example of how the descriptions of L2 language have benefited from LCR is the English Profile project, a large-scale project based on the Cambridge Learner Corpus and aimed at describing the characteristics of learner English in terms of different linguistic features found in L2 learners' exam scripts rated according to the proficiency descriptors from the CEFR (www.englishprofile.org/). Since the project included both the analysis of vocabulary and grammar (English Vocabulary Profile, EVP, and English Grammar Profile, EGP; for details see Capel, 2012 and O'Keeffe & Mark, 2017, respectively), it was possible to describe different features of learner language, including words and phraseological units (e.g., collocations or phrasal verbs) that characterise language use across specific topics and proficiency levels (see Figure 5 for examples of B1-level phrasal verbs related to the topic of communication).

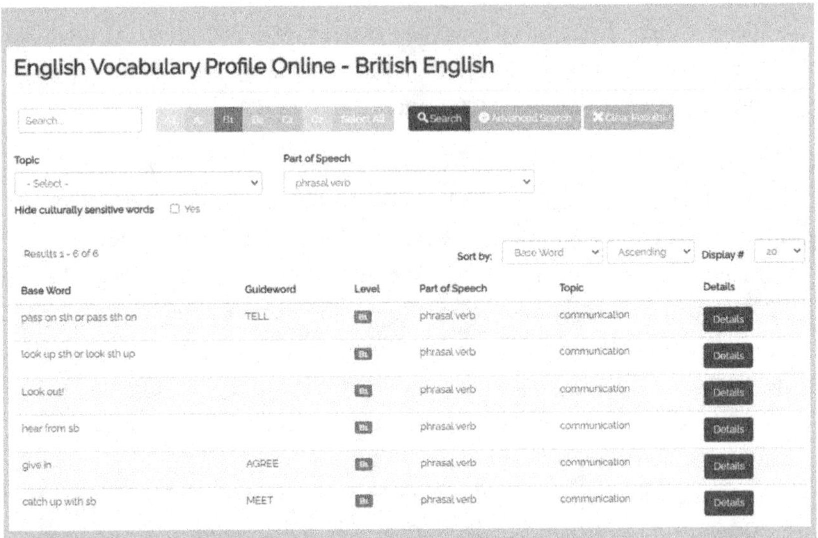

English Vocabulary Profile Online - British English

Figure 5 Sample English Profile output for B1-level phrasal verbs related to the topic of communication

CEFRLex (https://cental.uclouvain.be/cefrlex/) is another example of a web-based resource that relies on corpus and computational tools and shows word frequency distributions for six main European languages. For English, for instance, the resource describes the use of 15,280 words and collocations (normalised frequencies) and maps them onto the CEFR proficiency levels (see Dürlich & François, 2018 for a full account). Such corpus-based resources are a valuable addition to the toolkit available to researchers, language teachers and practitioners. In addition to informing SLA theory and helping to quantify the construct of L2 proficiency, they are also important pedagogically, providing new ways of describing the lexical and phraseological competence of L2 learners (see Leńko-Szymańska, 2015 for an example of how the English Vocabulary Profile was used to rate and assess samples of L2 learner production).

The same can be seen in corpus-based work into the collocational and phraseological sophistication of academic language. In addition to highlighting the role of register variation (Biber, 2009; Miller & Biber, 2015; Gablasova et al., 2017), much of this work has focused on measuring the extent to which L2 academic texts rely on collocations and phraseological patterning. An illustrative example of this research is O'Donnell et al.'s (2013) study which explored the presence of formulaic language (the number and quality of lexical bundles) in output produced by L1 and L2 writers (graduate and undergraduate students). Four corpus measures were used to tap into different dimensions of formulaic competence: frequencies of phrases (*n*-grams), their psycholinguistic coherence and salience as expressed by an association measure (MI scores), frequencies of phrase-frames (groupings of phrases which are identical except for one word in the same position as in 'it is good/interesting/useful/nice to do something') and native norms operationalised as the presence or absence of phrases from the Academic Formulas List (Simpson-Vlach & Ellis, 2010).

Results revealed that academic language was found to rely heavily on genre-specific formulas as well as a wide range of rhetorical expressions and constructions which help to build the structure of texts. As evidenced by significant differences in the writing produced by graduate and undergraduate students, formulas constituted the tools of the trade and effectively differentiated between expert and apprentice writing. Interestingly, the study reported largely no effects of the L1/L2 status, with both groups of writers exhibiting similar patterns in the deployment of academic phrases. These results indicate that it is not only L2 users who need to acquire phrasal vocabulary to be able to function effectively in academic discourse or other professional registers. Academic writing is a skill that needs crafting, also in the case for L1 users who develop this kind of competence over time and as a result of practice, which is of relevance to language pedagogy and the delivery of language courses focused on academic vocabulary and phraseology (e.g., EAP courses). The findings also have important methodological implications, suggesting that perhaps rather than relying on L1–L2 comparisons, corpus-based research might benefit more from making distinctions between novice versus expert academic users regardless of their L1 status.

Finally, findings of corpus-based studies into L2 lexical and collocational sophistication need to refer to the role of input L2 learners receive. What is known from SLA research is that the amount of language exposure is of fundamental importance to L2 learning, with the quantity and quality of words and phrases produced by L2 users lending themselves easily to corpus analysis. For instance, such analyses can examine an increased use of lower-frequency words or changes in collocation use over time as learners progressively get exposed to more L2 input. In this line of research, L1 corpora such as COCA have traditionally been treated as a proxy for language experience. However, by definition, such corpora can only be an approximation of the experience of L2 learners, with learner or pedagogic corpora being more likely to serve as a window into L2 learning and use. Two studies by Northbrook and Conklin (2018; 2019) are an excellent example of this, using a bespoke corpus of L2-English teaching materials from Japan. With this pedagogic corpus accurately representing the type of language L2 learners are typically exposed to, the findings pointed to important differences in the distribution of lexical bundles (e.g., 'I want to'; 'a lot of') in the L2 corpus versus the L1 reference corpus (Northbrook & Conklin, 2018). Further, the authors found that it was frequency information retrieved from the pedagogic corpus that drove L2 learners' processing of such bundles in a phrasal judgement task (Northbrook & Conklin, 2019), confirming the role of classroom materials in determining much of L2 learning.

While focused on lexical bundles, these results have clear implications for collocations studies. In line with usage-based approaches to language learning, they make a strong case for the application of learner- or context-relevant corpora as a basis for claims about the acquisition of both single-word and phrasal vocabulary. A similar call has been made by Myles and Cordier (2017), who argue that assumptions about L2 learners' use of formulaic sequences should not be made based on findings drawn from L1 corpora. This is because L1 users' formulaic sensitivity and intuitions about collocations likely vary, with the formulaic repertoire of particular speakers or writers tending to reflect their own language experience and idiosyncratic 'formulalects'. With L2 exposure being much more varied and individualised, this is even more the case, for as already shown in Section 4.2.2, L2 learners' tallying of statistical information on collocations and phraseological patterning is contingent on a whole range of different factors.

To recap, the discussion in this subsection has clearly demonstrated how the knowledge of collocations, similarly to the knowledge of individual words, manifests itself in the richness and sophistication of L2 texts, with L2 collocational competence lending itself to quantification by means of corpus-based metrics or tests. Further, this overview has also shown how the number and quality of collocations found in learner output can serve as a reflection or marker of proficiency growth, particularly when studies of L2 acquisition takes place in different contexts. Collectively, these findings make important contributions in terms of deepening our theoretical understanding of the complex ways L2 collocations are acquired. This research is also important practically, informing how L2 collocational knowledge can be enhanced through the process of teaching. A range of teaching-related aspects of L2 collocation studies are discussed in the following section.

4.3 Applied Corpus Linguistics: Corpora for Teaching L2 Collocations

As this Element is concerned with the use of corpus methods for analysing the learning and use of L2 collocations, the discussion in this final section addresses what has become known as applied corpus linguistics. This is a strand of research that focuses on the applications of corpora to solve practical problems across diverse fields (for useful examples, see Römer, 2022 or *Applied Corpus*

Linguistics, a recently launched specialised journal devoted to this area). One of them is the area of language education and L2 pedagogy, where the importance of collocations has been on the increase, recognising the role of phraseology and phrasal vocabulary in L2 learning and teaching.

> **Quote 13**
> Carter (2012, p. 2) 'The shift in emphasis from the single word to collocations to pairs or groups of words as integrated chunks of meaning and usage have now become a much more fully accepted aspect of vocabulary description and pedagogy. Clearly, for the learner of any second or foreign language too, learning the ways in which words form chunks is not a luxury; such patterning permeates even the most basic, frequent words and is needed for successful communication.'

It is beyond the scope of this Element to review an ever-increasing body of corpus-based phraseology literature on a wide variety of topics pertinent to L2 pedagogy (for a comprehensive overview of the use of corpora in English language teaching and learning, see Jablonkai & Csomay, 2022; see also Szudarski, 2022 who specifically addresses the role of corpora in teaching L2 vocabulary and phraseology). Instead, what follows is a summary of the main trends within practically oriented corpus-based work as relevant to L2 collocation studies. First, indirect uses of corpora are presented (Section 4.3.1), followed by a discussion of corpus-based lists of collocations (Section 4.3.2), L2 teaching resources (Section 4.3.3) and data-driven learning focused on L2 phraseology (Section 4.3.4).

4.3.1 Indirect Impact of Corpora on Teaching L2 Collocations

Generally speaking, the applications of corpus analysis in practically oriented L2 research can be discussed under two main categories: indirect and direct uses of corpora (Römer, 2011; Szudarski, 2022). The former refers to the use of corpus findings to select pedagogically relevant vocabulary, create lexically oriented teaching materials and raise L2 learners' awareness of single-word and phrasal vocabulary (see Jones & Durrant, 2021 for a useful discussion of corpus-based teaching materials targeting vocabulary). The latter, the direct use of corpora in the classroom, concerns data-driven learning (DDL), where corpus analysis is treated as a teaching technique involving the presentation of corpus data (e.g., concordances for specific collocations analysed during classes). This distinction is useful for discussing the impact of corpus linguistics on L2 pedagogy, thus the paragraphs that follow address these topics one by one, focusing on issues relevant to teaching L2 collocations.

Firstly, corpus-based investigations of language use and vocabulary in particular have been instrumental in describing and selecting specific linguistic features to be included in L2 instruction (e.g., differences between high- and low-frequency words or collocations in general vs. academic English). A case in point is lexical profiling enabled by tools such as VocabProfile (www.lextutor.ca/vp/comp/) or AntWordProfiler (www.laurenceanthony.net/software/antwordprofiler/), both of which allow us to analyse texts by looking at the proportions of words at specific frequency levels (e.g., VocabProfile provides Paul Nation's 1,000-word bandings based on BNC/COCA data, which can be used as a reference corpus in this analysis).

For collocations specifically, the www.wordandphrase.info/ interface embedded within the COCA corpus (www.english-corpora.org/coca/) is a particularly useful tool (see Figure 6). Similarly to VocabProfile or AntWordProfiler, one functionality of this web-based tool is highlighting different types of words in uploaded texts (e.g., high-frequency vs. low-frequency as determined by COCA). Crucially, it also enables us to carry out powerful and detailed searches on selected phrases found in a given text (e.g., finding similar collocates from the same part of speech or synonyms). This means that the interface functions as a collocational thesaurus, using corpus evidence to discover examples of relevant phrases and providing a wealth of qualitative and quantitative insights.

More pedagogically oriented corpus-based tools which operate in a similar way include the English Vocabulary Profile (already mentioned in Section 4.2.4) or Pearson's Global Scale of English Teacher Toolkit (www.pearson.com/english/about-us/global-scale-of-english.html). The latter is

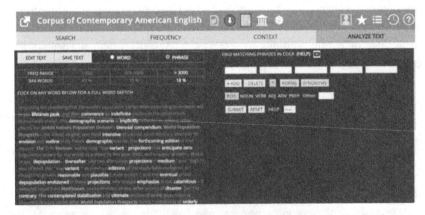

Figure 6 Output from a frequency-based analysis of a sample academic text using www.wordandphrase.info

a reference tool based on a corpus analysis of a large number of L2 texts, resulting in a scale (from 10 to 90) aimed at enabling accurate measurement and description of L2 learner progress at different proficiency levels. For instance, focusing on the four main language skills, the tool assists with the selection of specific language features, be it vocabulary or grammar, needed by L2 learners to move from one proficiency level to the next (for details on the methodology used to identify level-appropriate words and phrases, see Benigno & de Jong, 2016).

Such examples clearly illustrate how corpus findings can be effectively integrated into L2 pedagogy, helping to assess the pedagogical value of single-word and phrasal vocabulary. A highly relevant study that demonstrates how to implement this process in classroom conditions has been described by He and Godfroid (2019). Details of their design and findings are presented in Study Box 9.

STUDY BOX 9

He and Godfroid (2019)

Background & Aims: The study provides a useful example of how to combine corpus-derived and pedagogical information (teachers' ratings) to select context-specific vocabulary. Namely, using frequency, usefulness and difficulty as key criteria for the identification of academic words and phrases, the authors sought to determine how these features could be combined together as a novel method of prioritising academic vocabulary to be targeted on an intensive L2 English programme. The proposed step-by-step procedure was tested empirically (by means of a cluster analysis; discussed in the following), resulting in pedagogically relevant groupings of lexical items based on both linguistic and pedagogic factors.

Research Question(s)

1. What is the frequency, usefulness and difficulty profile of the target vocabulary (words and collocations) in an upper-intermediate pre-university L2 English course?

2. Can this vocabulary be assigned to different groupings as a way of prioritising it for teaching based on criteria such as frequency, usefulness and difficulty?

Methodology

- One hundred and eighty-nine target items: 165 single words ('abandon', 'confine') and 24 phrases, including collocations ('take issue with', 'immune system'), prepositional phrases ('in jeopardy') or phrasal verbs ('pop up')

- All target items rated by 76 experienced L2 English instructors in terms of usefulness and difficulty (seven-point scales) and frequency (COCA and its academic section)
- Combining all this data, a cluster analysis revealed five distinct clusters of vocabulary varying in terms of frequency, usefulness and difficulty; for each of these properties, a high, medium and low level was distinguished
- Cluster 1, for instance, contained vocabulary with low frequency, low usefulness and medium difficulty (e.g., 'skyrocket'), while Cluster 5 grouped items that were highly frequent, useful and of lowest difficulty (e.g., 'consequence')
- Pedagogical recommendations made, showing how such groupings of academic vocabulary can be prioritised for L2 teaching

Findings & discussion: Results indicated an interesting set of correlations between frequency, usefulness and difficulty as the three criteria determining the pedagogical relevance of L2 vocabulary. Interestingly, as regards collocations, while the relationship between frequency and usefulness was significant, the levels of difficulty (as rated by L2 teachers) did not correlate either with frequency or usefulness. Intuitively, these results make sense because difficult or infrequent items are unlikely to be rated as more useful or learnable units. Rather, it is high-frequency lexis that is typically considered to be easier to learn, with the caveat that more common items may also prove challenging in L2 learning (e.g., collocations with high-frequency verbs 'make' or 'take'). Such results therefore point to the value of combining objective corpus-based frequency data with more subjective but context-relevant pedagogical information (in this case, teachers' ratings of vocabulary to be taught on an academic English course). In terms of implications, based on the study, the authors called for prioritising highly frequent and useful vocabulary with low difficulty (Cluster 1), arguing that such vocabulary provides a better return for learning efforts and consequently is worth targeting through explicit L2 teaching. In turn, low-frequency and difficult items with low usefulness were assigned the lowest pedagogical priority, with L2 teachers being encouraged to replace such difficult items with more frequent ones that help optimise L2 vocabulary instruction.

Naturally, these are only recommendations based on findings from one setting (an American university) and more research is warranted across other learning contexts and vocabulary types (e.g., technical collocations) before any generalisations can be offered. Nevertheless, the study's main contribution is that it demonstrates how, thanks to the integration of corpus and teaching insights, L2 vocabulary can be usefully described by means of multiple metrics of lexical difficulty as well as pedagogical considerations. Further, similarly to Martinez (2013) discussed in Study Box 6, the proposed protocol provides an empirically derived method for dealing with the multiplicity of single-word and phrasal vocabulary, effectively filtering it for specific teaching contexts and learners' language needs.

Further examples of the indirect impact of corpora on teaching L2 vocabulary can be found in the area of language syllabus design and materials development. In these contexts, corpus insights have played a key role in increasing the visibility of collocations and formulaic language more broadly, informing teachers' and materials writers' decisions about the inclusion and presentation of phrasal vocabulary in teaching materials (see chapter 6 in Szudarski, 2018 for a detailed discussion). Crucially, the adoption of more lexically oriented teaching approaches that highlight the role of collocations in L2 learning is closely related to how far corpus findings influence language pedagogy and whether publishers and coursebook writers make use of corpus evidence while designing new teaching materials. In this respect, more studies such as Curry et al. (2022) are needed to facilitate dialogue in which publishers, editors and individual authors of L2 teaching resources turn to corpora as a source of pedagogically valid information. Specifically, Curry et al. (2022) demonstrate how corpus-based research into the changing frequencies of specific lexical items (in this case, spoken English adverbs such as 'literally' or 'so') can inform the work of publishers and ensure that the materials they create reflect the changing nature of language and highlight the most frequent features (be it adverbs, collocations or other relevant features). The study is a perfect illustration of the indirect implications of corpus research on L2 pedagogy, showing how to narrow the gap between research and teaching practice (Chambers, 2019) and deliver research-informed L2 teaching.

4.3.2 Corpus-Based Lists of Collocations

The development of corpus-based lists of collocations is another area where the impact of corpora has been instrumental. Being aware of the sheer number of collocations and difficulties in acquiring them in the L2 on the one hand and the impossibility of addressing all of them through explicit classroom instruction on the other, a great deal of applied corpus research has attempted to produce lists of the most useful or error-prone L2 phraseology. This has been particularly visible in research focusing on academic collocations (e.g., the Academic Collocation List by Ackermann & Chen, 2013 or the Academic English Collocation List by Lei & Liu, 2018). This section describes the key aspects of this work, using one representative study as a model of good practice.

Conceptualised as additional teaching materials that enhance L2 learning, such lists of collocations are typically based on specific corpus-derived measures (e.g., raw frequencies, log-likelihood or MI scores) and pedagogical criteria (e.g., teachers' ratings of utility or learnability). Simpson-Vlach and Ellis's (2010) Academic Formulas Lists (AFL) is an exemplary design in this regard and while it focuses on statistically based lexical bundles rather than collocations, it is highly relevant to the present discussion. Namely, it shows how to draw insights from multiple sources of data and provides extended evidence for the selection of pedagogically relevant academic phraseology. Study Box 10 outlines the methodology and main findings of this study.

Study Box 10

Simpson-Vlach and Ellis (2010)

Background & Aims: The aim of Simpson-Vlach and Ellis was to use several corpora (details to follow) to identify the most prominent examples of formulaic phrases found in academic language. The importance of these phrases was determined by comparing academic and non-academic texts, based on criteria such as frequency (10 occurrences per million was the minimum frequency of all target phrases) or statistical significance (log likelihood was used to compare frequencies between academic and non-academic texts). Crucially, the study went beyond this corpus analysis, with the selection of phrases also informed by L2 instructors' pedagogical judgement.

Research Question(s): To what extent are corpus metrics and teachers' ratings useful for deriving a pedagogically useful list of academic phraseology?

Methodology
- Corpora used: Michigan Corpus of Academic Spoken English, BNC and Ken Hyland's corpus of research papers
- Recognising the role of register variation, speech and writing data analysed separately
- Corpus-based analysis accompanied by expert-based ratings of pedagogical utility of phrases ('formula teaching worth' provided by EAP professionals)

Findings & Discussion: The resultant Academic Formulas List (AFL) is comprised of three versions: a core version of 207 academic phrases used frequent in both speech and writing (e.g., 'in terms of', 'as well as', 'on the basis'), a version of the 200 most frequent spoken phrases and a version of the 200 most frequent written phrases. As regards language pedagogy, covering over 200 phrases still requires substantial efforts in terms of instruction in L2 phraseology, but the prospect of targeting a limited set of context-relevant phrases is less daunting. Further, given this evidence-based selection, the process seems more manageable for L2 teachers, empowering them to decide themselves which phrases to focus on. Naturally, how these phrases should be taught largely depends on the learning needs of particular students and what pedagogical methods are chosen; this could be, for instance, grouping of phrases according to linguistic features (e.g., collocations formed around nouns) or discourse functions ('to some extent', expressing stance, or 'in the context of', as a referential expression). Crucially, in addition to these pedagogical insights, the AFL has also made an important methodological contribution. Thanks to its innovative and multi-pronged design, the list has been employed in subsequent studies, spurring new research and serving as a proxy for English academic phraseology (see Omidian et al., 2022 or Wingrove, 2022, where AFL assisted the quantification of academic phraseology in L2 output).

It should be added that there are many more examples of corpus-derived lists of phraseology, and judging by the number of new publications in this area, this trend is likely to continue (see also Nguyen & Coxhead, 2022 for a recent proposal on how to evaluate the pedagogical value of corpus-based lists of collocations). This growing body of research is a positive sign which indicates how the study of collocations and phraseology has been enhanced by the availability of corpora and how collocations and other important phrases can be promoted in L2 pedagogy. However, with so many new lists being developed, attention must also be paid to the validity of such corpus-derived resources (Schmitt & Schmitt, 2020), keeping in mind that they should be constructed for particular purposes and particular groups of L2 learners.

4.3.3 Corpus- and Technology-Enhanced L2 Teaching Resources

Positive changes as regards the indirect influence of corpus findings on teaching and learning L2 collocations have resulted in the creation of a new generation of technology-enhanced teaching aids and tools. In particular, these are tools that draw on the affordances and functionalities of computer-assisted language learning (CALL; for useful discussions of CALL-informed resources and approaches to formulaic language, see Cobb, 2019 and Meunier, 2020). For the purposes of this section, only a brief reference is made to Lin (2022) and Frankenberg-Garcia et al. (2019) as examples of cutting-edge corpus-based teaching resources aimed at promoting collocational and phraseological knowledge.

Lin's (2022) project concerns IdiomsTube as the first-ever CALL tool that employs YouTube videos as a way of facilitating the learning of English formulaic phrases. At the time of writing, the tool is based on 53,635 idiomatic expressions verified by their presence in reputable dictionaries, but there is certainly scope for crowdsourcing more examples. IdiomsTube is designed in such a way that it assesses the lexical difficulty of user-selected videos, identifies useful items (the criterion being the frequency of idiomatic expressions in captions that accompany YouTube videos), generates automatic learning tasks that target the phrases in question and finally recommends more videos with similar content reflecting learners' search history. While not without its challenges (e.g., determining priorities in selecting phrases, the presence of phrases in videos of varying length, deciding how many phrases should be targeted without overwhelming the user), such personalised, gamified and interactive tools hold a lot of pedagogical potential, particularly as the landscape of education is currently changing and L2 users spend increasingly more time in online environments (Cobb, 2019). Since Lin's tool is still in its early stages, more research is clearly warranted to examine its effectiveness across different L2 learning contexts. But the proposed design is a useful demonstration of how research findings from corpus analysis can be translated into practical L2 classroom-oriented solutions, providing learners with engaging learning materials and raising their collocational awareness.

Another example of such technology-enhanced L2 research which draws on corpus analysis is ColloCaid (Frankenberg-Garcia et al., 2019). Conceptualised as a digital text editor that makes real-time collocation suggestions as L2 learners produce academic writing, ColloCaid is a responsive tool which uses corpus-derived information on common phrases found in learner language and provides possible collocations or potential miscollocations around specific words (see Figure 7 for possible examples of collocations around the word 'report'). By presenting such examples, the tool heightens learners' collocational awareness and alerts them to any potential phraseological infelicities that might occur during the process of 'live' L2 writing.

Similarly to IdiomsTube, the effectiveness of ColloCaid is likely to depend on many factors (e.g., learners' proficiency and autonomy, essay topic, length of text), meaning that more research is needed to explore the effects and

Figure 7 ColloCaid output with possible collocations around the word 'report'

pedagogical affordances of such CALL-enhanced learning on L2 collocational gains. Nevertheless, such corpus-informed resources and bespoke pedagogical corpora (e.g., see Green, 2022 for a detailed discussion of the use of specialist ESP corpora for teaching collocations) exemplify the essence of applied phraseological research, adding to the toolbox of teachers and language practitioners working across a variety of L2 learning contexts.

4.3.4 Data-Driven Learning and Collocations

Last but not least, the applications of corpora in L2 collocation studies need to be discussed in relation to data-driven learning (DDL), which is the direct use of corpus data in language teaching and teacher training. There is a sizeable body of work (see Boulton & Vyatkina, 2021 for an overview) which shows how corpus data can be applied directly in the classroom for a range of pedagogical purposes (e.g., promoting more student-centred forms of language practice and enhancing the learning of specific linguistic features such as collocations). As demonstrated by two meta-analyses of research in this area (see Boulton & Cobb, 2017 and Lee et al., 2019), corpus data can serve as a basis for successful L2 classroom instruction in both single-word and phrasal vocabulary.

> **Quote 14**
> Boulton and Cobb (2017, p. 386) 'DLL [data-driven learning] works pretty well in almost any context where it has been extensively tried.'

Admittedly, most DDL research to date has been conducted in university-level L2 learners, but a recent volume edited by Crosthwaite (2020) convincingly shows how DDL can also be implemented successfully with younger and lower-level learners. As regards collocations and phraseology, Szudarski (2020) is a good instance of a classroom intervention based on the use of concordances from the BNC which targeted fifteen pedagogically relevant phrases (e.g., 'by far' or 'straight away'; all of them were taken from the PHRASE list published by Martinez & Schmitt, 2012). The study found that such a DDL approach was more effective than a more traditional dictionary-based form of teaching in terms of enhancing L2 learners' phraseological knowledge. Interestingly, however, qualitative insights from both learners and teachers also indicated that DDL, as a completely new way of approaching L2 instruction, required a change in their thinking and behaviour, pointing to important pedagogical challenges associated with the introduction of corpus analysis to lower-level students.

Further, while research shows that DDL can work as an effective form of teaching L2 collocations, its implementation and effectiveness depend to a large extent on the corpus literacy of language teachers, as well as their pedagogical capabilities and readiness to adopt new teaching approaches in their classrooms. This of course is closely linked to teacher education and training that is essential in terms of explaining the mechanics of corpus analysis (Leńko-Szymańska, 2022). Given teachers' busy schedules, a focus on improving their corpus literacy should certainly be an important part of the ongoing efforts aimed at bridging the gap between corpus research and practice (Chambers, 2019). In fact, this challenge is often mentioned in both collocation studies and applied corpus research more broadly, as an aspect that requires greater attention. More work is also needed to explore the full pedagogical spectrum of such student-centred approaches, in terms of examining what practical modifications should be introduced in the classroom to allow a more effective implementation of corpus analysis for L2 learning purposes. From the extant research (e.g., see Lee et al., 2020 for a model which takes into account learner variables in the use of DDL for L2 vocabulary learning), it is evident that there is room for corpus-informed L2 language teaching, capitalising on the wealth of information provided by corpora and drawing L2 learners' attention to collocations (see Viana, 2022 for many teaching suggestions and tested examples of corpus-informed lesson plans).

5 Conclusion and Avenues for Future Research

5.1 Corpus Revolution and Developments in Collocation Research

The aim of this Element has been to offer a comprehensive account of L2 collocation research as conducted, enhanced and informed by means of corpus analysis. Focusing in particular on the learning and use of collocations in the L2, the discussion has revolved around the mechanics of collocation analysis, the main issues and challenges associated with defining and identifying specific examples of collocations and the facilitative role of corpora in revealing the most prominent and pedagogically valid pairs of co-occurring words.

It is not an exaggeration to say that corpus-derived information has transformed the ways in which linguistic research is currently carried out. In fact, some authors have gone as far as calling the recent decades of linguistic work as a corpus revolution (e.g., Hanks, 2012; Chambers, 2019). This is well illustrated by O'Keeffe and McCarthy's (2022) chapter, which opens the second edition of the *Routledge Handbook of Corpus Linguistics*. In this discussion, the authors reflect upon changes in the design and use of corpora in the past decade and explain how the field has evolved since the publication of the first edition of their handbook. For instance, some indications of how the field has progressed include technological advancement, easier access to corpora (e.g., web-based corpus interfaces) and improved capabilities of corpus-based tools (e.g., as shown in Section 4.3.3, ColloCaid is a convincing example of such a tool related to L2 teaching). Further, O'Keeffe and McCarthy (2022, p. 3) also stress a rapid development of corpora in response to major political and social events such as Covid-19 or Brexit, with examples of databases such as the Coronavirus Corpus (part of the www.English-corpora.com interface) or the Brexit Corpus (available via Sketch Engine, www.sketchengine.eu/). Such corpora constitute a new type of rapid-response corpora and as a repository of human thought, they create avenues for new research into numerous changes observed in language use.

By way of example, Davies (2021) usefully explains how the Coronavirus Corpus can be used to analyse collocations around specific words in the quickly changing discourses around the Covid-19 pandemic. Thanks to the way the corpus is constructed, it is possible to analyse the frequencies of words and phrases and compare their use over time, even over such short periods as ten-day increments, which may be of particular relevance for time-sensitive and discourse-oriented studies of language use supported by corpus analysis. For instance, in terms of frequent collocates of the word 'mask', at the beginning of the pandemic (March 2020), language use seemed to have revolved around ensuring sufficient supplies of masks (e.g., high frequency of collocations such as 'making/donating/distributing masks'). However, as time went by (June 2020), the focus of the discourse shifted and concentrated more on wearing masks and introducing requirements to do so (e.g., a noticeably higher frequency of collocates such as 'wear', 'required' or 'encouraged').

The evolution of corpus linguistics is also evident in the types of language data and the ways in which it is collected. With increased volumes of digital and technology-enables communication that currently characterises our everyday life, no longer can we employ older dichotomies between written and spoken language. It is clear that e-language, particularly the use of language on social media and in online environments such as Zoom or Microsoft Teams, has now emerged as a separate category. From the perspective of language description then, such new domains of language open up possibilities for innovative research, including the analysis of collocations, their learning and use across diverse domains and settings.

In this context, studies such as Adolphs et al. (2020) and Lin (2022) are illustrative examples of how crowdsourcing and data crunching from the Internet are becoming popular methods of conducting linguistic research. For instance, Adolphs et al. (2020) focus on the opportunities and challenges associated with the use of smartphones as a way of recording linguistic information from individual speakers and using it develop context-specific lists of useful phraseology (e.g., phrases such as 'key figure', 'make sense' and 'long term' that are frequently found in academic lectures). While not without certain limitations (e.g., participants' confidence levels in reporting such data or reluctance to add new phrases to the list), there is clearly potential for scaling up such methods and collecting data that is authentic and context-specific. Another aspect of the evolution of corpus analysis is the tools we use, with Anthony's (2022) new version of AntConc serving as an example of software that innovatively ranks concordances based on the frequency of salient patterns rather than presenting them in the customary alphabetical order. Such developments hold a lot of potential and should facilitate the identification and interpretation of lexical and grammatical co-occurrence patterns, enabling the generation of fresh insights into the collocability of words.

Finally, given the focus of this Element on methodological matters, another aspect worth bearing in mind is the quality of corpus research and the importance of linguistic description and interpretation in corpus-based work. Many authors have recently underscored the fundamental importance of linguistic description, pointing to a sustained focus on language issues as a sine qua non if corpus analysis is to maintain its relevance and integrity in terms of analysing and interpreting the data that is available in corpora (Egbert et al., 2020; Larsson et al., 2022; O'Keeffe & McCarthy, 2022).

Quote 15
O'Keeffe and McCarthy (2022, p. 6) 'The persuasiveness of our arguments about language depends on the plausible and robust interpretation of the principled empirical evidence which the data throw up.'

As discussed in Section 3, linguistic description and interpretation should always take precedence over the choice of statistical tests, with research questions themselves dictating the choice of appropriate and 'minimally sufficient' procedures (Egbert et al., 2020, p. 39). As recently observed by Larsson et al. (2022, p. 153) in relation to the shifting nature of corpus research over the last decade, 'the greater the focus on statistical reporting, the more likely it is for language and linguistic analysis to get backgrounded'. Collocation research is no exception in this regard and for this reason, throughout this Element, there has been a consistent emphasis on the importance of and transparency in the formulation of research goals, the application of replicable criteria in defining collocations and the responsibility of the individual analyst to clearly describe the linguistic and methodological basis on which their claims are made.

5.2 Future Avenues for Collocation Research

Building on the current state of knowledge and findings reviewed throughout this Element, this section provides recommendations for future collocation research, as well as predictions how this line of inquiry might develop in the coming years. Empirical work into corpus-based phraseology is still rather young as a subfield within linguistics, with many questions remaining unanswered, particularly in studies based on learner corpora (Granger, 2019; 2021). However, considering the ubiquity of collocations and their importance for successful L2 learning and use, it can be safely stated that this strand of research is likely to grow. There are a number of directions in which this work can be taken:

1. Group versus individual perspective on collocational development

One interesting avenue to explore in the future is a group versus individual perspective on L2 collocational development (Forsberg Lundell, 2021). Given the nature of corpora, most LCR work to date has focused on aggregate data, without paying much attention to variation in collocation learning at the level of individual learners. However, 'nothing prevents learner corpora from being used as a basis for the study of individual trajectories' (Granger, 2019, p. 241), with a lot of potential for studies that combine corpus analysis with case studies or experimental data (e.g., Li & Schmitt, 2009; see also Bell, 2009 as an excellent example of a longitudinal case study into lexical L2 learning; see also Point 2 on mixed methods). On a theoretical level, rather than treating learner language as a deficient version of L1 use and focusing predominantly on L2 errors, one can observe a discernible change of thinking in LCR and SLA more broadly, homing in on what learners of a given language can do or achieve and how lexis, collocations and other features reflect this competence (e.g., see Capel, 2012). More research along these lines is encouraged, particularly with learners of languages other than English.

2. Mixed-methods and interdisciplinary research

Another direction in which corpus-based research is likely to develop is the increased use of mixed-methods and interdisciplinary designs, where authors draw on multiple sources of data (e.g., corpus findings, experimental data, classroom-based interventions). To a large extent, this is already happening, as attested to by studies where corpus insights and psycholinguistic findings complement each other, resulting in innovative methodologies that are better at capturing the complexity of learning L2 collocational knowledge (e.g., Öksüz et al., 2021; see also Römer, 2016 for an excellent discussion of the benefits of collaboration in corpus-based phraseological research). Likewise, as evidenced in Section 4.3, corpus findings can be usefully applied to inform L2 instruction, materials development and syllabus design, helping to identify context-appropriate examples of collocations and underline the role of phraseology as a key component of linguistic competence.

3. Replication studies

More attention in future corpus research should be devoted to replication efforts (Tracy-Ventura et al., 2021; Granger, 2019). Replication studies have been underused in many disciplines, including linguistics (Marsden et al., 2018), but are necessary to enable comparisons, draw more generalisable conclusions and increase the reproducibility of findings. As regards research into collocations and formulaicity, Lu et al. (2018) is an example of a replication study that extended O'Donnell et al.'s (2013) findings into the presence of formulaic language in academic writing. By focusing on the effects of different measures on the identification of phrases and considering the role of criterial consistency (i.e., the selection of corpora and specific criteria as the basis for this identification), Lu et al.'s study clearly demonstrates the benefits afforded by the refinement of previous methodologies. Specifically, while their findings support O'Donnell et al.'s original conclusion, they also underline the importance of using multiple corpus-based measures in identifying formulaic phrases and shed new light on the role of register variation in applying arbitrary thresholds for collocation measures such as MI. To borrow Granger's (2019, p. 251) apt words, 'in a field that involves so many variables, replication studies are essential'.

While in SLA there has been an increased focus on replication and multisite studies (see Peters et al., under review, as an example of a replication multisite design into incidental learning of L2 collocations), this trend has perhaps been less visible in corpus linguistics. Efforts in this regard need to be intensified as a way of enabling more comparisons across studies and reproducing findings across different learning contexts. Such steps are likely to 'strengthen the contribution' of corpus-based studies (Granger 2019, p. 242) to this quickly developing area of research and the collective understanding of the acquisition of formulaic units. In this context, it is also worth emphasising Miller and Biber's (2015) plea to underscore the role of corpus design in vocabulary research as a key factor that affects the validity of claims and corpus-based findings. In relation to phraseology and lists of common collocations, Miller and Biber observe how little attention researchers have paid to the influence of corpus design on the similarity and consistency of phraseological units retrieved from different corpora (e.g., collocations or lexical bundles). Because phrases are composed of both content and function words, it might be that the reliability of corpus-derived phrase lists is less adversely affected by corpus design and topic variation than lists of individual words (Miller & Biber, 2015, p. 50). This is of course an empirical question that should be addressed by future research. In particular, attention should be paid to the stability of lexical lists across different types of corpora (e.g., see Nguyen & Coxhead's 2022 interesting comparison of the Academic Collocation List (ACL) and the Academic English Collocation List (AECL) showing little overlap between the two lists).

4. Bridging the gap between research and practice

It is also clear that bridging the gap between corpus research and L2 learning and teaching practice remains a challenge (Chambers, 2019; O'Keeffe, 2021), and more work needs to be done to ensure that findings from corpus-based studies inform language instruction and translate into better solutions for the L2 classroom. For instance, while the research reviewed in this Element suggests that collocations are an important aspect of L2 proficiency and their presence affects the ratings of learner language, there is still little consensus on how to best teach different types of collocations and optimise their acquisition in the L2 (see Pellicer-Sanchez & Boers, 2019 for an over-view of pedagogical approaches to formulaic language). What is required is a more principled and research-informed approach to teaching both single-word and phrasal vocabulary, with more attention devoted to classroom instruction and teaching materials as the key source of input for L2 learners. In this sense, more studies such as Curry et al. (2022) are encouraged, because it is only by collaboration and an increased dialogue between corpus linguists on the one hand and publishers, coursebook writers, teachers and, crucially, language learners on the other that better language education can be delivered.

It is also imperative that the momentum is kept with research into corpus-based lists of collocations, teaching resources and user-friendly corpus interfaces that can be utilised to promote the knowledge of L2 phraseology. This is where research areas such as CALL and DDL have much to contribute, with technology-based tools enhancing the experience of L2 learning and helping to create the optimal classroom conditions for computer-assisted collocational learning (Cobb, 2019). Frankenberg-Garcia et al. (2019) and Lin (2022) discussed in Section 4.3.3 are a perfect example of what future CALL-based studies should focus on, showing the potential of corpus-based pedagogical tools, but examining also how such tools are perceived by language teachers and learners using them 'in the wild'.

This list of research priorities that merit attention is not exhaustive and many other examples could be added. However, considering the amount of new research that is currently available around the topic of collocations and the broader phenomenon of formulaic language, it is fair to say that the future of corpus research looks promising, making it particularly exciting to be working in this area of language studies.

5.3 Final Remarks

By way of conclusion, I would like to end this Element with some reflections that have accompanied the process of writing it. From the outset, this text has been conceptualised as a state-of-the-art review and synthesis of the field's current understanding of corpus-based collocation research. My intention has been to apply a critical eye to the ever-growing amount of work in this area and systematise the key findings in this strand of research. In terms of motivation to produce this kind of overview, I have been driven by a number of theoretical questions as well as methodological challenges that I have faced myself and kept returning to, either in the design of my own studies or while engaging with collocation work published by others. Examples of such recurring challenges are defining and identifying specific kinds of collocations, separating collocation pairs from other types of formulaic sequences, the multiplicity of factors that affect L2 collocational learning or assessing the validity and pedagogical relevance of corpus-derived lists of phraseological units. As pointed out by Wray (2019, p. 267), there are many variables to consider in the wide-ranging research that explores phraseological competence in the L2, and, given the inherent complexity of formulaicity as a linguistic phenomenon, insights can be drawn from the domains of cognition, social interaction, pragmatics and pedagogy, with no guarantee of finding simple answers to the research questions that are posed.

However, as emphasised throughout all the sections, it is abundantly clear that with the ongoing developments in the field of corpus linguistics, as well as the ease with which millions of words can currently be analysed, corpora do provide a whole range of options, tools and measures that enable data-based explorations and allow us to conduct analyses of the ways words collocate, what kinds of lexical or lexico-grammatical patterns they form and how such collocational pairs contribute to L2 learning and use. In this sense, Wray (2019) is right when she suggests that finding a single answer is far from the only purpose of the process of enquiry. Rather, the research process is very much about experimenting, drawing on different sources of information and 'increasing the intimacy of our knowledge of the phenomena that lie at the heart of our interest' (Wray, 2019, p. 267).

Hopefully, this is what this Element will do as well. I will feel my goals have been achieved if by highlighting the fundamental role of corpus linguistics in the study of collocations, this text contributes to the field's collective knowledge of the notion of collocations and their learning in the L2, inspires new research questions and generates further corpus-based findings in the fascinating area of linguistic inquiry.

References

Ackermann, K. & Chen, Y. H. (2013). Developing the Academic Collocation List (ACL): A corpus-driven and expert-judged approach. *Journal of English for Academic Purposes*, 12(4), 235–47. https://doi.org/10.1016/j.jeap.2013.08.002.

Adolphs, S., Knight, D., Smith, C. & Price, D. (2020). Crowdsourcing formulaic phrases: Towards a new type of spoken corpus. *Corpora*, 15(2), 141–68. https://doi.org/10.3366/cor.2020.0192.

Alderson, C. (2007). Judging the frequency of English words. *Applied Linguistics*, 28(3), 383–409. https://doi.org/10.1093/applin/amm024.

Altenberg, B. & Granger, S. (2001). The grammatical and lexical patterning of MAKE in native and non-native student writing. *Applied Linguistics*, 22(2), 173–95. https://doi.org/10.1093/applin/22.2.173.

Anthony, L. (2022). Addressing the challenges of data-driven learning through corpus tool design. Talk given as part of the International Perspectives on Corpora for Language Learning, University of Queensland, 29 April 2022.

Baker, P. (2016). The shapes of collocation. *International Journal of Corpus Linguistics*, 21(2), 139–164. https://doi.org/10.1075/ijcl.21.2.01bak.

Barfield, A. & Gyllstad, H., eds. (2009). *Researching Collocations in Another Language: Multiple Interpretations*. Basingstoke: Palgrave Macmillan.

Bell, H. (2009). The messy little details: A longitudinal case study of the emerging lexicon. In A. Barfield and T. Fitzpatrick, eds. *Lexical Processing in Second Language Learners: Papers and Perspectives in Honour of Paul Meara*. Bristol: Multilingual Matters, pp. 111–27.

Benigno, V. & de Jong, J. (2016). The 'Global Scale of English Learning Objectives for Young Learners': A CEFR-Based Inventory of Descriptors. In M. Nikolov, ed., *Assessing Young Learners of English: Global and Local Perspectives*. New York: Springer, pp. 43–64.

Biber, D. (2009). A corpus-driven approach to formulaic language in English: Multi-word patterns in speech and writing. *International Corpus of Corpus Linguistics*, 14(3), 275–311. https://doi.org/10.1075/ijcl.14.3.08bib.

Bley-Vroman, R. (1983). The comparative fallacy in interlanguage studies: The case of systematicity. *Language Learning*, 33, 1–17. https://doi.org/10.1111/j.1467-1770.1983.tb00983.x.

Boers, F., Eyckmans, J., Kappel, J., Stengers, H. & Demecheleer, M. (2006). Formulaic sequences and perceived oral proficiency: Putting a lexical approach to the test. *Language Teaching Research*, 10(3), 245–261. https://doi.org/10.1191/1362168806lr195oa.

Boone, G., De Wilde, V. & Eyckmans, J. (2022). A longitudinal study into learners' productive collocation knowledge in L2 German and factors affecting the learning. *Studies in Second Language Acquisition*, First view, 1–23. https://doi.org/10.1017/S0272263122000377.

Boulton, A. & Cobb, T. (2017). Corpus use in language learning: A meta-analysis. *Language Learning*, 67(2), 348–93. https://doi.org/10.1111/lang.12224.

Boulton, A. & Vyatkina, N. (2021). Thirty years of data-driven learning: Taking stock and charting new directions over time. *Language Learning & Technology*, 25(3), 66–89. http://hdl.handle.net/10125/73450.

Brezina, V. (2018). *Statistics in Corpus Linguistics. A Practical Guide.* Cambridge: Cambridge University Press.

Brezina, V. & Fox, L. (2021). Adjective + noun collocations in L2 and L1 speech: Evidence from the Trinity Lancaster Corpus and the Spoken BNC2014. In S. Granger, ed., *Perspectives on the L2 Phrasicon: The View from Learner Corpora*. Bristol: Multilingual Matters, pp. 152–77.

Brezina, V., McEnery, T. & Wattam, S. (2015). Collocations in contexts: A new perspective on collocation networks. *International Journal of Corpus Linguistics*, 20(2), 139–73. https://doi.org/10.1075/ijcl.20.2.01bre.

Capel, A. (2012). Completing the English Vocabulary Profile: C1 and C2 vocabulary. *English Profile Journal*, 3(1), 1–14. https://doi.org/10.1017/S2041536212000013.

Carrol, G. & Conklin, K. (2020). Is all formulaic language created equal? Unpacking the processing advantage for different types of formulaic sequences. *Language and Speech*, 63(1), 95–122. https://doi.org/10.1177/0023830918823230.

Carter, R. (2012). *Vocabulary: Applied Linguistic Perspectives*. London: Routledge.

Chambers, A. (2019). Towards the corpus revolution? Bridging the research–practice gap. *Language Teaching*, 52(4), 460–75.

Cobb, T. (2019). From corpus to CALL: The use of technology in teaching and learning formulaic language. In A. Siyanova-Chanturia & A. Pellicer-Sanchez, eds., *Understanding Formulaic Language: A second language acquisition perspective*. London: Routledge, pp. 192–210.

Cobb, T. & Horst, M. (2015). Learner corpora and phraseology. In S. Granger, G. Gilquin and F. Meunier, (eds., *Cambridge Handbook of Learner Corpus Research*. Cambridge: Cambridge University Press, pp. 185–206.

Conklin, K. (2020). Processing single-word and multiword items. In S. Webb, (ed., *Routledge Handbook of Vocabulary Studies*. London: Routledge, pp. 174–88.

Council of Europe (2001). *Common European Framework of Reference for Languages: Learning, teaching, assessment.* Cambridge: Cambridge University Press.

Cowie, A. P. (1994). Phraseology. In R. E. Asher, ed., *The Encyclopedia of Language and Linguistics.* Oxford: Pergamon, pp. 3168–71.

Crossley, S. A., Salsbury, T. & McNamara, D. S. (2015). Assessing lexical proficiency using analytic ratings: A case for collocation accuracy. *Applied Linguistics*, 36(5), 570–90. https://doi.org/10.1093/applin/amt056.

Crosthwaite, P., ed. (2020). *Data-Driven Learning for the Next Generation: Corpora and DDL for pre-tertiary learners.* London: Routledge.

Curry, N., Love, R. & Goodman, O. (2022). Adverbs on the move: Investigating publisher application of corpus research on recent language change to ELT coursebook development. *Corpora*, 17(1), 1–38. https://doi.org/10.3366/cor.2022.0233.

Davies, M. (2021). The Coronavirus Corpus: Design, construction, and use. *International Journal of Corpus Linguistics*, 26(4), 583–98.

Deng, Y. & Liu, D. (2022). A multi-dimensional comparison of the effectiveness and efficiency of association measures in collocation extraction. *International Journal of Corpus Linguistics*, 27(2), 191–219. https://doi.org/10.1075/ijcl.19111.den.

Durrant, P. (2014). Corpus frequency and second language learners' knowledge of collocations: A meta-analysis. *International Journal of Corpus Linguistics*, 19(4), 443–77.

Durrant, P. & Brenchley, M. (2022). The development of academic collocations in children's writing. In P. Szudarski & S. Barclay, eds., *Vocabulary Theory, Patterning and Teaching.* Bristol: Multilingual Matters, pp. 99–120.

Durrant, P. and Mathews-Aydinli, J. (2011). A function-first approach to identifying formulaic language in academic writing. *English for Specific Purposes*, 30, 58–72. https://doi.org/10.1016/j.esp.2010.05.002.

Durrant, P. & Schmitt, N. (2009). To what extent do native and non-native writers make use of collocations? *International Review of Applied Linguistics in Language Teaching*, 47(2), 157–77. https://doi.org/10.1515/iral.2009.007.

Durrant, P., Siyanova-Chanturia, A., Sonbul, S. & Kremmel, B. (2022). *Research Methods in Vocabulary Studies.* Amsterdam: John Benjamins.

Dürlich, L. and François, T. (2018). EFLLex: A Graded Lexical Resource for Learners of English as a Foreign Language. In Proceedings of the 11th International Conference on Language Resources and Evaluation (LREC 2018). Miyazaki, Japan, 7–12 May.

Egbert, J., Larsson, T. & Biber, D. (2020). *Doing Linguistics with a Corpus: Methodological considerations for the everyday user.* Cambridge: Cambridge University Press.

Ellis, N. (2002). Frequency effects in language processing: A review with implications for theories of implicit and explicit language acquisition. *Studies in Second Language Acquisition*, 24(2), 143–88. https://doi.org/10.1017/S0272263102002024.

Ellis, N. (2012). Formulaic language and second language acquisition: Zipf and the phrasal teddy bear. *Annual Review of Applied Linguistics*, 32, 17–44. https://doi.org/10.1017/S0267190512000025.

Ellis, N., Simpson-Vlach, R. & Maynard, C. (2008). Formulaic language in native and second language speakers: Psycholinguistics, corpus linguistics, and TESOL. *TESOL Quarterly*, 42(3),375–96. https://doi.org/10.1002/j.1545-7249.2008.tb00137.x.

Ellis, N., Simpson-Vlach, R., Römer, U., O'Donnell, M. & Wulff, S. (2015). Learner corpora and formulaic language in second language acquisition research. In S. Granger, G. Gilquin and F. Meunier, eds., *Cambridge Handbook of Learner Corpus Research*. Cambridge: Cambridge University Press, pp. 357–78.

Evert, S. (2009). Corpora and collocations. In A. Lüdeling and M. Kytö, eds., *Corpus linguistics: An International Handbook*, vol. 2. Berlin: Walter de Gruyter, pp. 1212–48.

Fernandez, J. & Davis, T. S. (2021). Overview of available learner corpora. In N. Tracy-Ventura and M. Paquot, eds., *The Routledge Handbook of Second Language Acquisition and Corpora*. New York: Routledge, pp. 145–57.

Firth, J. R. (1957). A synopsis of linguistic theory 1930–1955. In F. Palmer, ed., *Selected Papers of J. R. Firth 1952–1959*. London: Longman, pp. 168–205.

Fioravanti, I., Senaldi, M. S. G., Lenci, A. & Siyanova-Chanturia, A. (2021). Lexical fixedness and compositionality in L1 speakers' and L2 learners' intuitions about word combinations: Evidence from Italian. *Second Language Research*, 37(2), 291–322. https://doi.org/10.1177/0267658320941560.

Forsberg Lundell, F. (2021). Formulaicity. In N. Tracy-Ventura and M. Paquot, eds., *The Routledge Handbook of Second Language Acquisition and Corpora*. New York: Routledge, pp. 370–81.

Frankenberg-Garcia, A., Lew, R., Rees, G. et al. (2019). Developing a writing assistant to help EAP writers with collocations in real time. *ReCALL*, 31(10), 23–39. https://doi.org/10.1017/S0958344018000150.

Gablasova, D. (2021). Variability. In N. Tracy-Ventura and M. Paquot, eds., *The Routledge Handbook of Second Language Acquisition and Corpora*. New York: Routledge, pp. 358–69.

Gablasova, D., Brezina, V. & McEnery, T. (2017). Collocations in corpus-based language learning research: identifying, comparing and interpreting the evidence. *Language Learning*, 67, S1, 155–79. https://doi.org/10.1111/lang.12225.

Gabrielatos, K. (2018). Keyness analysis: Nature, metrics and techniques. In C. Taylor and A. Marchi, eds., *Corpus Approaches to Discourse: A Critical Review*. Oxford: Routledge, pp. 225–58.

Garcia-Salido, M., & Garcia, M. (2018). Comparing learners' and native speakers' use of collocations in written Spanish. *International Review of Applied Linguistics in Language Teaching*, 56(4), 401–26. https://doi.org/10.1515/iral-2016-0103.

Gilquin, G. (2021). Combining learner corpora and experimental methods. In N. Tracy-Ventura and M. Paquot, eds., *The Routledge Handbook of Second Language Acquisition and Corpora*. New York: Routledge, pp. 133–43.

Gilquin, G. (2022). One norm to rule them all? Corpus-derived norms in learner corpus research and foreign language teaching. *Language Teaching*, 55(1), 87–99. https://doi.org/10.1017/S0261444821000094.

Granger, S. (1996). From CA to CIA and back: An integrated approach to computerized bilingual and learner corpora. In K. Aijmer, B. Alteberg, & M. Johansson, eds., *Languages in contrast: Text-Based Cross-Linguistic Studies*. Lund: Lund University Press, pp. 37–51.

Granger, S. (2009). Learner corpora: A window onto the L2 phrasicon. In A. Barfield and H. Gyllstad, eds., *Research Collocations in Another Language*. Houndmills: Palgrave Macmillan, pp. 60–5.

Granger, S. (2012). How to use foreign and second language learner corpora. In A. Mackey and S. Gass, eds., *Research Methods in Second Language Acquisition: A Practical Guide*. Chichester: Blackwell Publishing, pp. 7–29.

Granger, S. (2015). Contrastive interlanguage analysis: A reappraisal. *International Journal of Learner Corpus Research*, 1(1), 7–24. https://doi.org/10.1075/ijlcr.1.1.01gra.

Granger, S. (2019). Formulaic sequences in learner corpora: Collocations and lexical bundles. In A. Siyanova-Chanturia and A. Pellicer-Sanchez, eds., *Understanding Formulaic Language: A Second Language Acquisition Perspective*. New York: Routledge, pp. 228–47.

Granger, S. (2021). Phraseology, corpora and L2 research. In S. Granger, ed., *Perspectives on the L2 Phrasicon: The View from Learner Corpora*. Bristol: Multilingual Matters, pp. 3–21.

Granger, S. & Bestgen, Y. (2014). The use of collocations by intermediate vs. advanced non-native writers: A bigram-based study. *Journal International*

Review of Applied Linguistics in Language Teaching, 52(3), 229–52. https:// doi-org.nottingham.idm.oclc.org/10.1515/iral-2014-0011.

Granger, S., Gilquin, G., & Meunier, F., eds. (2015). *The Cambridge Handbook of Learner Corpus Research*. Cambridge: Cambridge University Press.

Green, C. (2022). Corpora for teaching collocations in ESP. In R. R. Jablonkai and E. Csomay, eds., *The Routledge Handbook of Corpora in English Language Teaching*. London: Routledge, pp. 206–19.

Gries S.-Th. (2008). Phraseology and linguistic theory: a brief survey, in S. Granger & F. Meunier (eds.), *Phraseology: An Interdisciplinary Perspective*. Amsterdam: John Benjamins, 3–25.

Gries, S. Th. (2013). 50-something years of work on collocations. What is or should be next. *International Journal of Corpus Linguistics*, 18(1), 137–65. https://doi.org/10.1075/ijcl.18.1.09gri.

Gries, S. Th. (2015). Statistics for learner corpus research. In S. Granger, G. Gilquin and F. Meunier, eds., *Cambridge Handbook of Learner Corpus Research*. Cambridge: Cambridge University Press, pp. 159–81.

Gyllstad, H. & Wolter, B. (2016). Collocational processing in light of the phraseological Continuum Model: Does semantic transparency matter? *Language Learning*, 66(2), 296-323. https://doi.org/10.1111/ lang.12143.

Hanks, P. (2012). The corpus revolution in lexicography. *International Journal of Lexicography*, 25(4), 398–436. https://doi.org/10.1093/ijl/ecs026.

He, X. & Godfroid, A. (2019). Choosing words to teach: A novel method for vocabulary selection and its practical application. *TESOL Quarterly*, 53(2), 348–71. https://doi.org/10.1002/tesq.483.

Henriksen, B. (2013). Research on L2 learners' collocational competence and development: A progress report. In C. Bardel, B. Laufer, and C. Lindqvist, eds., *L2 Vocabulary Acquisition, Knowledge and Use*. EuroSLA: EuroSLA Monographs Series vol. 2, pp. 29–56.

Hoey, M. (2004). The textual priming of lexis. In G. Aston, S. Bernardini and D. Stewart, eds., *Corpora and Language Learners*. Amsterdam: John Benjamins, pp. 21–42.

Hoey, M. (2005). *Lexical Priming: A New Theory of Words and Language*. London: Routledge.

Howarth, P. (1996). *Phraseology in English Academic Writing*. Tubingen: Max Niemayer Verlag.

Howarth, P. (1998). Phraseology and second language proficiency. *Applied Linguistics*, 19(1), 24–44. https://doi.org/10.1093/applin/19.1.24.

Hunston, S. (2022). *Corpora in Applied Linguistics*. Cambridge: Cambridge University Press.

Jablonkai, R. R. & Csomay, E., eds. (2022). *The Routledge Handbook of Corpora in English Language Teaching*. London: Routledge.

Jenkins, J. & Leung, (2019). From mythical 'standard' to standard reality: The need for alternatives to standardized English language tests. *Language Teaching*, 52(1), 86–110. https://doi.org/10.1017/S0261444818000307.

Jones, M. & Durrant, P. (2021). What can a corpus tell us about vocabulary teaching materials? In A. O'Keeffe and M. McCarthy, eds., *Routledge Handbook of Corpus Linguistics*. London: Routledge, pp. 341–57.

Kecskes, I. (2019). Formulaic language and its place in intercultural pragmatics. In Siyanova-Chanturia, A. and Pellicer-Sanchez, A., eds., *Understanding Formulaic Language. A Second Language Acquisition Perspective*. London: Routledge, pp. 132–49.

Kilgariff, A., Baisa, V., Bušta, J. et al. (2014). The Sketch Engine: ten years on. *Lexicography ASIALEX*, 1, 7–36. https://doi.org/10.1007/s40607-014-0009-9.

Kjellmer, G. (1991). A mint of phrases. In K. Aijmer and B. Altenberg, eds., *English Corpus Linguistics: Studies in Honour of Jan Svartvik*. London: Longman, pp. 111–27.

Kyle, K. (2020). Measuring lexical richness. In S. Webb, ed., *Routledge Handbook of Vocabulary Studies*. London: Routledge, pp. 454–76.

Larsson, T., Egbert, J., & Biber, D. (2022). On the status of statistical reporting versus linguistic description in corpus linguistics: A ten-year perspective. *Corpora*, 17(1), 137–57. https://doi.org/10.3366/cor.2022.0238.

Laufer, B. & Waldman, T. (2011). Verb-noun collocations in second language writing: A corpus analysis of learners' English. *Language Learning*, 61(2), 647–72. https://doi.org/10.1111/j.1467-9922.2010.00621.x.

Le Bruyn B. & Paquot, M. (eds.) (2021). *Learner Corpus Research Meets Second Language Acquisition*. Cambridge: Cambridge University Press.

Lee, H., Warschauer, M., & Lee, H. L. (2019). The Effects of Corpus Use on Second Language Vocabulary Learning: A Multilevel Meta-analysis. *Applied Linguistics*, 40(5), 721–753. https://doi.org/10.1093/applin/amy012.

Lee, H., Warschauer, M. & Lee, J. H. (2020). Toward the establishment of a data-driven learning model: Role of learner factors in corpus-based second language vocabulary learning. *Modern Language Journal*, 104(2), 345–62. https://doi.org/10.1111/modl.12634.

Lei, L. & Liu, D. (2018). The academic English collocation list. *International Journal of Corpus Linguistics*, 23(2), 216–43. https://doi.org/10.1075/ijcl.16135.lei.

Leńko-Szymańska, A. (2015). The English Vocabulary Profile as a benchmark for assigning levels to learner corpus data. In M. Callies and S. Gotz, eds., *Learner Corpora in Language Testing and Assessment*. Amsterdam: John Benjamins, pp. 115–40.

Leńko-Szymańska, A. (2020). *Defining and Assessing Lexical Proficiency*. New York: Routledge.

Leńko-Szymańska, A. (2022). Training teachers and learners to use corpora. In R. R. Jablonkai and E. Csomay, eds., *The Routledge Handbook of Corpora in English Language Teaching*. London: Routledge, pp. 509–24.

Li, J. & Schmitt, N. (2009). The acquisition of lexical phrases in academic writing: A longitudinal case study. *Journal of Second Language Writing*, 18, 85–102. https://doi.org/10.1016/j.jslw.2009.02.001.

Lin, P. (2022). Developing an intelligent tool for computer-assisted formulaic language learning from YouTube videos. *ReCALL*, 34(2), 185–200. https://doi.org/10.1017/S0958344021000252.

Lu, X. (2022). *Corpus Linguistics and Second Language Acquisition: Perspectives, Issues, and Findings*. London: Routledge.

Lu, X., Kisselev, O., Yoon, J. & Amory, M. D. (2018). Investigating effects of criterial consistency, the diversity dimension, and threshold variation in formulaic language research: Extending the methodological considerations of O'Donnell et al. (2013). *International Journal of Corpus Linguistics*, 23 (2), 158–82. https://doi.org/10.1075/ijcl.16086.lu.

Malec, W. (2010). On the asymmetry of verb-noun collocations. In J. Arabski and A. Wojtaszek, eds., *Neurolinguistic and Psycholinguistic Perspectives on SLA*. Bristol: Multilingual Matters, pp. 126–44.

Marsden, E., Morgan-Short, K., Thompson, S., & Abugaber, D. (2018). Replication in second language research: Narrative and systematic reviews and recommendations for the field. *Language Learning*, 68(2), 321–91. https://doi.org/10.1111/lang.12286.

Martinez, R. (2013). A framework for the inclusion of multiword expressions in ELT. *ELT Journal*, 67(2), 184–198. https://doi.org/10.1093/elt/ccs100.

Martinez, R., & Schmitt, N. (2012). A phrasal expressions list. *Applied Linguistics*, 33(3), 299–320. https://doi.org/10.1093/applin/ams010.

Mautner, G. (2022). What can a corpus tell us about discourse? In A. O'Keeffe and M. McCarthy, eds., *Routledge Handbook of Corpus Linguistics*. London: Routledge, pp. 250–62.

McCallum, L. & Durrant, P. (2022). *Shaping writing grades. Collocation and writing context effects*. Cambridge: Cambridge University Press.

Meunier, F. (2020). Resources for learning multiword items. In S. Webb (Ed.), *Routledge handbook of vocabulary studies*. London: Routledge, pp. 336–50.

Miller, D. & Biber, D. (2015). Evaluating reliability in quantitative vocabulary studies. The influence of corpus design and composition. *International Journal of Corpus Linguistics*, 20(1), 30–53. https://doi.org/10.1075/ijcl.20.1.02mil.

Myles, F. & Cordier, C. (2017). Formulaic sequence (FS) cannot be an umbrella term in SLA: Focusing on psycholinguistic FSs and their identification. *Studies in Second Language Acquisition*, 39(1), 3–28. https://doi.org/10.1017/S027226311600036X.

Nesselhauf, N. (2003). The use of collocations by advanced learners of English and some implications for teaching. *Applied Linguistics*, 24(2), 223–42. https://doi.org/10.1093/applin/24.2.223.

Nguyen, T. M. H. & Coxhead, A. (2022). Evaluating multiword unit word lists for academic purposes. *ITL: International Journal of Applied Linguistics*, Online-first articles, 1–29. https://doi.org/10.1075/itl.21041.ngu.

Northbrook, J. & Conklin, K. (2018). 'What are you talking about?' An analysis of lexical bundles in Japanese junior high school textbooks. *International Journal of Corpus Linguistics*, 23(3), 311–34. https://doi.org/10.1075/ijcl.16024.nor.

Northbrook, J. & Conklin, C. (2019). Is what you put in what you get out? Textbook-derived lexical bundle processing in beginner English learners. *Applied Linguistics*, 40(5), 816–33. https://doi.org/10.1093/applin/amy027.

Oakey, D. (2022). What can a corpus tell us about lexis? In A. O'Keeffe and M. McCarthy, eds., *Routledge Handbook of Corpus Linguistics*. London: Routledge, pp. 185–203.

O'Donnell, M., Römer, U. & Ellis, N. (2013). The development of formulaic sequences in first and second language writing: Investigating effects of frequency, association, and native norm. *International Journal of Corpus Linguistics*, 18(1),83–108. https://doi.org/10.1075/ijcl.18.1.07odo.

O'Keeffe, A. (2021). Data-driven learning: A call for a broader research gaze. *Language Teaching*, 54(2), 259–72. https://doi.org/10.1017/S0261444820000245.

O'Keeffe, A. & Mark, G. (2017). The English Grammar Profile of learner competence: Methodology and key findings. *International Journal of Corpus Linguistics*, 22(4), 457–89. https://doi.org/10.1075/ijcl.14086.oke.

O'Keeffe, A. & McCarthy, M. (2022). 'Of what is past, or passing, or to come': corpus linguistics, changes and challenges. In A. O'Keeffe and M. McCarthy, eds., *Routledge Handbook of Corpus Linguistics*. London: Routledge, pp. 1–9.

O'Keeffe, A., McCarthy, M. & Carter, R. (2007). *From Corpus to Classroom*. Cambridge: Cambridge University Press.

Öksüz, D., Brezina, V. & Rebuschat. P. (2021). Collocational processing in L1 and L2: The effects of word frequency, collocational frequency, and association. *Language Learning*, 71(1), 55–98. https://doi.org/10.1111/lang.12427.

Omidian, T., Siyanova-Chanturia, A. & Durrant, P. (2022). Predicting parameters of variation in the use of academic multiword expressions in university student writing. In P. Szudarski & S. Barclay, eds., *Vocabulary Theory, Patterning and Teaching*. Bristol: Multilingual Matters, pp. 141–66.

Omidian, T., Siyanova-Chanturia, A., & Spina, S. (2021). Development of formulaic knowledge in learner writing: A longitudinal perspective. In S. Granger, ed., *Perspectives on the L2 Phrasicon: The View from Learner Corpora*. Bristol: Multilingual Matters, pp. 178–205.

Partington, A. (2004). Utterly content in each other's company: Semantic prosody and semantic preference. *International Journal of Corpus Linguistics*, 9(1), 131–56. https://doi.org/10.1075/ijcl.9.1.07par.

Paquot, M. (2018). Phraseological competence: A missing component in university entrance language tests? Insights from a study of EFL learners' use of statistical collocations. *Language Assessment Quarterly*, 15(1), 29–43. https://doi.org/10.1080/15434303.2017.1405421.

Paquot, M. (2019). The phraseological dimension in interlanguage complexity research. *Second Language Research*, 35(1), 121–45. https://doi.org/10.1177/0267658317694221.

Paquot, M. & Granger, S. (2012). Formulaic language in learner corpora. *Annual Review of Applied Linguistics*, 32, 130–49. https://doi.org/10.1017/S0267190512000098.

Pawley, A. & Syder, F. H. (1983). Two puzzles for linguistic theory: Nativelike selection and nativelike fluency. In J. C. Richards and R. W. Schmidt, eds., *Language and Communication*. London: Longman, pp. 191–225.

Pellicer-Sanchez, A. & Boers, F. (2019). Pedagogical approaches to the teaching and learning of formulaic language. In Siyanova-Chanturia, A. and Pellicer-Sanchez, A., eds., *Understanding Formulaic Language: A Second Language Acquisition Perspective*. London: Routledge, pp. 153–73.

Pellicer-Sanchez, A., Vilkaitė-Lozdienė, & Siyanova-Chanturia, A. (2022). Examining L2 learners' confidence of collocational knowledge. In P. Szudarski & S. Barclay, eds., *Vocabulary Theory, Patterning and Teaching*. Bristol: Multilingual Matters, pp.121–40.

Pérez-Paredes, P., Mark, G. & O´Keeffe, A. (2020). *The Impact of Usage-Based Approaches on Second Language Learning and Teaching*. Cambridge: Cambridge University Press.

Peters, A. M. (1983). *The Units of Language Acquisition*. Cambridge: Cambridge University Press.

Peters, E., Puimege, E. & Szudarski, P. (under review). Repetition and incidental learning of multiword units: A conceptual replication study of Webb, Newton, and Chang (2013). *Language Learning.*

Pitzl, M.-L. (2018). *Creativity in English as a Lingua Franca: Idiom and Metaphor.* Boston: De Gruyter Mouton.

Römer, U. (2009). Corpus research and practice: What help do teachers need and what can we offer? In K. Aijmer, ed., *Corpora and Language Teaching.* Amsterdam: John Benjamins, pp. 83–98.

Römer, U. (2011). Corpus research applications in second language teaching. *Annual Review of Applied Linguistics*, 31, 205–25. https://doi.org/10.1017/S0267190511000055.

Römer, U. (2016). Teaming up and mixing methods: Collaborative and cross-disciplinary work in corpus research on phraseology. *Corpora*, 11(1), 113–29. https://doi.org/10.3366/cor.2016.0087.

Römer, U. (2022). Applied corpus linguistics for language acquisition, pedagogy, and beyond. *Language Teaching*, 55(2), 233–44. https://doi.org/10.1017/S0261444821000392.

Rubin, R., Housen, A., & Paquot, M. (2021). Phraseological complexity as an index of L2 Dutch writing proficiency: A partial replication study. In S. Granger, ed., *Perspectives on the L2 Phrasicon: The View from Learner Corpora.* Bristol: Multilingual Matters, pp. 101–25.

Saito, K. (2020). Multi- or single-word units? The role of collocation use in comprehensible and contextually appropriate second language speech. *Language Learning*, 70(2), 548–88. https://doi.org/10.1111/lang.12387.

Schmitt, N. (2010). *Researching Vocabulary: A Vocabulary Research Manual.* New York: Palgrave Macmillan.

Schmitt, N. (2019). Understanding vocabulary acquisition, instruction, and assessment: A research agenda. *Language Teaching*, 52(2), 261–74. https://doi.org/10.1017/S0261444819000053.

Schmitt, N. (2022). Norbert Schmitt's essential bookshelf: Formulaic language. *Language Teaching*, 1–12. https://doi.org/10.1017/S0261444822000039.

Schmitt, N. & Carter, R. (2004). Formulaic sequences in action: An introduction. In N. Schmitt, ed., *Formulaic Sequences: Acquisition, Processing, and Use.* Philadelphia: John Benjamins Press, pp. 1–22.

Schmitt, N. & Dunham, B. (1999). Exploring native and non-native intuitions of word frequency. *Second Language Research*, 15(2), 389–411. https://doi.org/10.1191/026765899669633186.

Schmitt, N. & Schmitt, N. (2020). *Vocabulary in Language Teaching.* Cambridge: Cambridge University Press.

Shi, J., Peng, G. & Li, D. (2023). Figurativeness matters in the second language processing of collocations: Evidence from a self-paced reading experiment. *Language Learning*, 73(1), 1–37. https://doi.org/10.1111/lang.12516.

Simpson-Vlach, R. & Ellis, N. (2010). An Academic Formulas List: New methods in phraseology research. *Applied Linguistics*, 31(4), 487–512. https://doi.org/10.1093/applin/amp058.

Sinclair, J. (1991). *Corpus, Concordance, Collocation: Describing English Language*. Oxford: Oxford University Press.

Sinclair, J. (2004). *Trust the Text: Language, Corpus and Discourse*. London: Routledge.

Sinclair, J., Jones, S. & Daley, R. (2004). *English Collocation Studies: The OSTI Report*. London: Bloomsbury.

Siyanova-Chanturia, A. & Omidian, T. (2020). Key issues in researching multi-word items. In S. Webb, ed., *Routledge Handbook of Vocabulary Studies*. London: Routledge, pp. 529–44.

Siyanova-Chanturia, A. & Pellicer-Sanchez, A., eds. (2019). *Understanding Formulaic Language: A Second Language Acquisition Perspective*. London: Routledge.

Siyanova-Chanturia, A. & Spina, S. (2015). Investigation of native speaker and second language learner intuition of collocation frequency. *Language Learning*, 65(3), 533–62. https://doi.org/10.1111/lang.12125.

Siyanova-Chanturia, A. & Spina, F. (2020). Multi-word expressions in second language writing: A large-scale longitudinal learner corpus study. *Language Learning*, 70(2), 420–63. https://doi.org/10.1111/lang.12383.

Sonbul, S. & El-Dakhs, D. (2020). Timed versus untimed recognition of L2 collocations: Does estimated proficiency modulate congruency effects? *Applied Psycholinguistics*, 41(5), 1197–222. https://doi.org/10.1017/S0142716420000051X.

Stubbs, M. (2009). The search for units of meaning: Sinclair on empirical semantics. *Applied Linguistics*, 30(1), 115–37. https://doi.org/10.1093/applin/amn052.

Szudarski, P. (2017). Learning and teaching L2 collocations: Insights from research. *TESL Canada Journal*, 34(3), 205–16. https://doi.org/10.18806/tesl.v34i3.128.

Szudarski, P. (2018). *Corpus Linguistics for Vocabulary: A Guide for Research*. London: Routledge.

Szudarski, P. (2020). Effects of data-driven learning on enhancing the phraseological knowledge of secondary school learners of L2 English. In P. Crosthwaite, ed., *Data-Driven Learning for the Next Generation: Corpora and DDL for Pre-tertiary Learners*. London: Routledge, pp. 133–49.

Szudarski, P., (2022). Corpora and teaching vocabulary and phraseology. In R. R. Jablonkai and E. Csomay, eds., *The Routledge Handbook of Corpora in English Language Teaching*. London: Routledge, pp. 41–55.

Szudarski, P. & Barclay, S., eds. (2022). *Vocabulary Theory, Patterning and Teaching*. Bristol: Multilingual Matters.

Szudarski, P., & Carter, R. (2016). The role of input flood and input enhancement in EFL learners' acquisition of collocations. *International Journal of Applied Linguistics*, 26(2), 245–65. https://doi.org/10.1111/ijal.12092.

Szudarski, P. & Conklin, K. (2014). Short- and long-term effects of rote rehearsal on ESL learners' processing of L2 collocations. *TESOL Quarterly*, 48(4), 833–42. https://doi.org/10.1002/tesq.201.

Tracy-Ventura, N., Paquot, M. & Myles, F. (2021). The future of corpora in SLA. In N. Tracy-Ventura and M. Paquot, eds., *The Routledge Handbook of Second Language Acquisition and Corpora*. New York: Routledge, pp. 409–24.

Viana, V. (ed.) (2022). *Teaching English with Corpora: A Resource Book*. London: Routledge.

Vilkaitė, L. (2016). Are nonadjacent collocations processed faster? *Journal of Experimental Psychology: Learning, Memory and Cognition*, 42, 1632–42. https://doi.org/10.1037/xlm0000259.

Vilkaitė, L. & Schmitt, N. (2019). Reading collocations in an L2: Do collocation processing benefits extend to non-adjacent collocations? *Applied Linguistics*, 40(2), 329–354. https://doi.org/10.1093/applin/amx030.

Vilkaitė-Lozdienė, L. & Conklin, K. (2021). Word order effect in processing collocations. *The Mental Lexicon*, 16(2–3), 362–96. https://doi.org/10.1075/ml.20022.vil.

Webb, S., Newton, J., & Chang, A. C. S. (2013). Incidental learning of collocation. *Language Learning*, 63(1), 91–120. https://doi.org/10.1111/j.1467-9922.2012.00729.x.

Wingrove, P. (2022). Measuring the frequency of the academic formulas list across corpora: A case study based in TED talks and Yale lectures. *Applied Corpus Linguistics*, 2(1), 1–11. https://doi.org/10.1016/j.acorp.2021.100012.

Wolter, B. & Gyllstad, H. (2013). Frequency of input and L2 collocational processing. A comparison of congruent and incongruent collocations. *Studies in Second Language Acquisition*, 35(3), 451–82. https://doi.org/10.1017/S0272263113000107.

Wolter, B. & Yamashita, J. (2018). Word frequency, collocational frequency, L1 congruency, and proficiency in L2 collocational processing: What accounts for L2 performance? *Studies in Second Language Acquisition*, 40(2), 395–416. https://doi.org/10.1017/S0272263117000237.

Wood, D. (2020). Classifying and identifying formulaic language. In S. Webb, ed., *Routledge Handbook of Vocabulary Studies*. London: Routledge, pp. 30–45.

Wray, A. (2002). *Formulaic Language and the Lexicon*. Cambridge: Cambridge University Press.

Wray, A. (2019). Concluding question: Why don't second language learners more proactively target formulaic sequences? In A. Siyanova-Chanturia and A. Pellicer-Sanchez, eds., *Understanding Formulaic Language: A Second Language Acquisition Perspective*. London: Routledge, pp. 248–69.

Cambridge Elements ≡

Corpus Linguistics

Susan Hunston
University of Birmingham

Professor of English Language at the University of Birmingham, UK. She has been involved in Corpus Linguistics for many years and has written extensively on corpora, discourse, and the lexis-grammar interface. She is probably best known as the author of *Corpora in Applied Linguistics* (2002, Cambridge University Press). Susan is currently co-editor, with Carol Chapelle, of the Cambridge Applied Linguistics series.

Advisory Board

About the Series

Corpus Linguistics has grown to become part of the mainstream of Linguistics and Applied Linguistics, as well as being used as an adjunct to other forms of discourse analysis in a variety of fields. It continues to become increasingly complex, both in terms of the methods it uses and in relation to the theoretical concepts it engages with. The Cambridge Elements in Corpus Linguistics series has been designed to meet the needs of both students and researchers who need to keep up with this changing field. The series includes introductions to the main topic areas by experts in the field as well as accounts of the latest ideas and developments by leading researchers.

Cambridge Elements $\equiv$

Corpus Linguistics

Elements in the Series

Multimodal News Analysis across Cultures
Helen Caple, Changpeng Huan and Monika Bednarek

*Doing Linguistics with a Corpus: Methodological Considerations
for the Everyday User*
Jesse Egbert, Tove Larsson and Douglas Biber

Citations in Interdisciplinary Research Articles
Natalia Muguiro

Conducting Sentiment Analysis
Lei Lei and Dilin Liu

Natural Language Processing for Corpus Linguistics
Jonathan Dunn

The Impact of Everyday Language Change on the Practices of Visual Artists
Darryl Hocking

*Analysing Language, Sex and Age in a Corpus of Patient Feedback: A Comparison of
Approaches*
Paul Baker and Gavin Brookes

Shaping Writing Grades: Collocation and Writing Context Effects
Lee McCallum and Philip Durrant

Corpus-Assisted Discourse Studies
Mathew Gillings, Gerlinde Mautner and Paul Baker

Collocations, Corpora and Language Learning
Paweł Szudarski

A full series listing is available at: www.cambridge.org/corpuslinguistics